The Sexy Bitch's Book

of

Finding him, Doing him

and

Dating him

The Sexy Bitch's Book of Finding him, Doing him and Dating him

SIOBHAN KELLY

Ulysses Press

Published in the United States by
Ulysses Press
P.O. Box 3440
Berkeley, CA 94703
www.ulyssespress.com

ISBN 1-56975-446-2
Library of Congress Control Number: 2004108864

First published as *Searching for Sex in the City* in Great Britain
in 2003 by Ebury Press, Random House.

Printed in Canada by Transcontinental Printing

1 3 5 7 9 8 6 4 2

Cover artwork: gettyimages.com
Cover design: Leslie Henriques

Distributed in the U.S.A. by Publishers Group West

contents

introduction

searching for sex...

If you're the kind of girl who spends a fortune on foxy shoes and then half that much money again every week on cabs because you can't really walk anywhere in them, if you get withdrawal symptoms when you go more than two minutes away from a Starbucks and, most importantly of all, if you're scanning that sea of faces for your *him*—the guy to whisk you off your feet, melt your heart and make all your dreams come true (or at the very least give you dinner and an orgasm, although hopefully not at the same time), then you, my friend, are officially a Sexy Bitch. And this book is for you. Think of it as the last weapon in your dating armory—it's as essential as your cell phone, your little black book or, indeed, your little black panties when it comes to tracking down a guy who's hot enough to handle you.

Why do you need this book? Unless you've been hanging out in a convent your whole life—the fact that you're reading a book with the words "sexy" and "bitch" in the title suggests you ain't no Reverend Mother—you'll have noticed that dating today is complicated, cutthroat and confusing. Climbing the promotion ladder, interesting shopping opportunities and trying to fit in time to see your friends leaves little time for searching for sex—and when you do have the time, you're usually too exhausted to put the necessary effort into finding out where the single, up-for-it guys are. And that's where I come in. I'm here to take you through every stage of the dating game, from the sort of underwear you need to the best pick-up joints to the perfect cafe for that post-date postmortem.

I'm also here to solve the dating dilemmas that confound even the sassiest of sexy bitches. Like, when he asks for your number, which of the gazillion ways of contacting you should you give out? Work, cell, home, email, pager, fax, carrier pigeon? What if you're sharing a cab home and you live at opposite ends of town? Is it still OK if the guy pays? If he holds the door open for you, does that make him chivalrous or a chauvinist? Is it really true that neglecting to shave your legs and wearing your period panties guarantees you'll get laid, while spending $100 in Victoria's Secrets means the date will end in a chaste cheek kiss? Kinky sex games on the first date: yes or no? These are the burning questions that need to be addressed.

We are raised with the idea that Saturday night is date night from the moment the braces come off our teeth, but what is dating really all about today? Well, nice girls date because they want to find a nice boy to settle down and get married to. Poor old nice girls: Someone ought to tell them that the 1950s are over. Sexy bitches, on the other hand, know that dating is as much about networking and having a good time and getting to know new people as it is about getting laid (although, hey, if that happens, it's a bonus).

The sexy bitch regards dating as a sport as much as a way to form relationships. She espies her prey, puts time and effort into the hunt and knows that the thrill of the chase and the pre-date preparation is half the fun. She knows that sitting around looking cute on a barstool, waiting for a guy to notice her, won't get her anywhere apart from a place alone in the taxi line at the end of the night: the sexy bitch's keyword is proactivity, but she works smarter, not harder. Follow the rules in my book and you'll learn how to chase a guy so he thinks he's the one running around after you. And after a couple of dates, he will be.

I know from whence I speak: It goes without saying that I'm a bonafide sexy bitch with the engagement ring, the coordinating underwear and the sex-induced muscle sprains to prove it. But before my beau came along, I went on lots of dates and met lots of men. A lot of the men I saw while I was a singleton, if that doesn't sound like too much of a contradiction in terms, I went out with for the right reasons. Example: I genuinely liked a lot of them—they made me laugh and had nice arms. A couple of them I went out with for the wrong reasons. Example: the man who had recently been dumped by a famous soap opera actress—I thought if I hung around long enough some of the glamour might rub off on me. A lot of these men have since passed into legend among me and my girlfriends. Some for the right reasons—the man who swept me off my feet into his James Bond–style sports car and took me to some of the best hotels and restaurants in London—and some for the wrong reasons, like the hill-billy pesticide salesman who came to pick me up in his tractor, or the poor unfortunate who turned up at my front door wearing a leather tie with a piano key motif and in doing so unwittingly signed his own death warrant. Men came and went (mostly in that order).

I also spent four years working on a women's magazine and have read more books on the psychology of dating and interviewed more relationship counselors and psychologists than you've had hot dates. And perhaps most important of all, I'm fortunate enough to be surrounded by a fabulous support network of sexy bitches: girl-friends in every stage of the dating game, from die-hard singletons to married with kids on the way. I've enlisted the help of all these people and I've consulted some additional experts, from dating gurus to psy-chosexual psychologists, to strippers to stylists to personal shoppers.

Just as a hunter wouldn't dream of going on safari without a map, a gun and a nice beige suit, you shouldn't even think about dating until you've read this book from cover to cover. Read on and find out you how to negotiate the minefield in your Jimmy Choo stilettos. You'll be an expert on snagging eligible bachelors before you can say "gotcha.

1 the man map

where to find those darned elusive eligible bachelors

The most commonly asked question by singletons is, "Where the freakin' hell are all the single, gorgeous men?" Well, I've got news for you: In the same way it's said we're never more than 20 feet away from rats in downtown New York, sexy bitches are never more than a few minutes away from an eligible bachelor. They're all out there, somewhere, staring into the bottom of their glasses and saying to their friends, "Where the freakin' hell are all the single, gorgeous women?"

As with real estate, location is everything: You just need to find exactly where they are and when they're going to be there. You just need a little insider knowledge to pin 'em down, that's all.

For sexy bitches, anywhere from the parking lot to the ATM machine and from the park to the gym is a potential pick-up joint, but there are places that offer greater-than-average odds of you meeting a man. And here they are:

traditional pick-up joints

Traditional pick-up joints are basically places with a license to serve alcohol that also play music.

bars

The boundaries between bar, club and restaurant are blurring: Your local neighborhood bar may have a dance floor and serve Asian food until dawn. Most good bars combine eating, drinking and dancing, ensuring that your pick-up style (whatever that may be) is catered for. Lots of singletons say they don't understand why they don't meet men when they spend half their lives knocking back the Pinot Grigio in upscale bars with their girlfriends. Are you sitting comfortably? That's why it ain't working. Girls tend to sit down while they drink while men prefer to prop themselves up at the bar. There are several reasons for this, chiefly the way girly shoes make your feet hurt, and the fact that men like to take up as much space as possible while they're sinking beers. It makes them feel important. That's why those big-city wine bars with blond wood tables and huge windows seem great in theory, but in practice are only good for meeting men on a Friday night when it's so full there's nowhere to sit and *everybody* stands up and mingles. It's hard for men to cross the great divide: No matter how transfixed he is by your beauty, he's going to have to be very brave to overcome the physical and psychological obstacle of a table packed with screaming girlies. Try sitting at bar stools next time you're out and be astonished by how much more male attention you get.

clubs

Clubs are excellent places to pick up guys because they're pretty dark, most of the occupants are very drunk, and the dance floor is a great icebreaker and forum for parading yourself in front of all the boys. There's an atmosphere of anything goes and people are up for adventure (or at the very least a French kiss at the end of the night).

One mistake a lot of urban singletons make is heading for the biggest club in the middle of town. This is a bad idea because any city is going to attract tourists in droves, and men on vacation generally lack imagination and head for the biggest, tackiest joint in town. While this is fine if your idea of fun is a screamed conversation over cheesy dance tunes and a one-night stand at a gross out-of-town motel, it's not a great place to form any kind of lasting relationship.

As a rule of thumb, the smaller, hipper, more obscure and newer the club, the better your chances are of finding a man who a) will call you later in the week, and b) you will want to talk to when he does. The more specialized the music, the greater likelihood any man you see is not there to look for a lady but to enjoy himself and relax with his friends—which, ironically, makes any conquest much more likely to stay the course. Scour your local listings for upcoming DJs, theme nights and new openings.

Taken to its most fabulous extreme are nightclubs with exorbitant cover charges. Hard to get into (being able to foot the entrance fee isn't enough—you have to dress just right and possess a certain *je ne sais quois*), but very exciting once you're there, they range from the fabulously exclusive (by which I mean the kind of joint that "looks after" Robert de Niro and his superstar kind when they're in town) to the more user-friendly, localized clubs. People at these clubs are likely to have a bit of money behind them (which is handy if you need someone to buy your Cosmopolitans for you, having blown half a month's salary at the door alone). And because the same people go there time after time on a regular basis, they're also fabulous places to network because they're full of fabulous people, and the more fabulous people you meet, the more fabulous men you have potential to be introduced to.

dive bar

I'm talking about that dubious bar with the flashing neon sign outside that looks like it should be in the ass of nowhere somewhere just outside Homersville but that has somehow wound up in the big city. These are the bars that sexy bitches tend to walk past very quickly, but don't dismiss them quite yet. Pros: lots of men, cheap drinks. Cons: a lot of the men will remind you of your dad and you'll be picking up your own bar tab. If it's glamorous clientele and men in Armani power suits you're after, keep walking. But if you want a down-to-earth night out that might, just might, end up with you meeting a down-to-earth man, then take a deep breath and cross that threshold. Employ the 20-second rule: People may well be unused to the presence of a sexy bitch in their dive bar so it's only natural that they'll look up from their Buds. But if after 20 seconds you feel incredibly uncomfortable and the only lady present looks like she's been selling her body since 1975, turn on your kitten heel and get the hell outta there—not being able to see into most dive bars means you take your chances every time you walk into one. But I reckon that only

---

TIP

Learn to play pool. Not only do the boys get an eye-popping view of your cleavage when you lean over, people gathered around a pool table inevitably strike up some kind of witty, sparkling conversation. If you've got a knack for the game and you become a hustler, they'll think that's incredibly sexy. If you can't get the hang of it and sink the white ball your first time, every time, they'll just use it as an excuse to stand behind you and give you a quick feel while you scratch the ball.

adds to the excitement and spirit of adventure. Once you've established that this is a fun, friendly kinda place, there is only one stipulation I must make: It must have a pool table.

weddings and parties

Parties are fabulous and reliable places to meet men because your friends have great taste (otherwise they wouldn't be hanging with you, right?). The only problems arise when you've been single for a couple of years and have met all the single men in your social circle. Which is why you should contrive to get yourself invited to as many weddings as possible. There will be a singletons table and the atmosphere is so charged with romance that the most unlikely pairings occur. And if all your friends are having such fun being single there are no weddings on the horizon, crash one. Look through your city's paper for wedding announcements, call the church pretending you've lost your invitation and find out where the party is. By half past nine during the reception, no one can see straight anyway and the happy couple—the only ones who will be able to identify you as a crasher—should be halfway to their honeymoon (although if the only male attention you get is the father of the bride grabbing your waist a little too tightly during the conga, you might want to call it a night).

21st-century pick-up joints

Cities are awash with places that are less obvious but utterly appropriate places to find that special someone. And no, it doesn't just happen this way in the movies.

Twenty-first-century pick-up joints are, in my opinion, a better place to meet men if you want a lasting relationship. Once we stop thinking along the lines of "Where can I go to pick up guys?" and start thinking in terms of "Where can I go to enjoy myself?" we'll forgo the usual guy-hunting circuit in favor of an experience that will be a reward in itself.

This works on so many levels. For starters, if your mission is to meet men, and only to meet men, you'll ooze desperation and they can smell it, you know. Men won't want to come near you and, if your mission fails, you'll come home depressed with nothing to show for your time and money—not even good memories.

If you're genuinely engaged by your surroundings, you'll be relaxed, happy and stimulated, your guard will be down, and men will flock to you. Let me give you some examples: I have been asked out by a man I'd known for about half an hour at the top of the Harbour Bridge in Sydney, Australia. I was wearing overalls, a gray sweatshirt and a beanie hat with a light attached. Typical pick-up gear it was most definitely not, but I was having the time of my life. Andreas—that was his name—said he was attracted to me by the fact I'd gone up the bridge all on my own and was still whooping my head off and chatting with strangers. Although I was traveling solo, I had a boyfriend at home so I had to say no—but the fact he'd approached me at all was a revelation.

On a more successful note, my friend Sarah took a job in Belfast, Northern Ireland, where she didn't really know anyone. To fill her weekends, she joined her local Conservation Volunteers project. It's not every girl that wants to spend her weekends wearing waders and fishing garbage (including syringes and used condoms) out of a gross, polluted urban stream, but it worked for Sarah. Because she was so enthusiastic about the task at hand, meeting men was the last thing on her mind and her personality shone through. Before the first month was over, she'd been asked out by more tree-huggers than she could shake a (made-from-sustainable-forest) stick at. Another friend, Donna, is a real foodie and would go to the ends of the earth in her quest for the perfect organic sun-blushed tomato. She's now living with a man who used to work at her local deli. They'd been debating the merits of tahini versus tsatsiki for nearly a year before he casually mentioned a spare ticket he had for an organic cheese-and-wine-tasting evening. They just recently bought a plot of endangered Australian rainforest together.

gyms

Avoid a gym that doesn't offer classes and only has the basic running machines and weight training. These tend to be cliquey and it's very hard to find common areas to socialize in. Exclusive corporate gyms tend to attract the kind of man who looks after his health; any place called "Sweat Til Your Eyes Bleed" should be avoided like the plague.

Personal trainers are your most valuable resource: Not only will they whip you into shape, thus making you more confident and alluring, it's also advisable to befriend one and ask him/her to find out what times the object of your desire trains and what classes he takes. The con is that he'll see you sweating, red and panting with your hair plastered to your head, but this is far outweighed by the pros: If he likes you looking like that, he'll love you forever, and the fitter he is, the longer he'll be able to keep going in the sack. And that can only be a good thing.

cafes

You can find a man in a cafe in one of two ways—because urban singletons are such creatures of routine, you're likely to see the same person buying the same coffee day in, day out every morning before work. Get the staff on your side: Starbucks is great but has a high turnover of staff that might not remember everyone they serve. So try to get your caffeine fix in a less corporate, more independent cafe. Flirt with the 50-something Italian guy who works the espresso machine (every cafe worth its chocolate-dipped biscotti should have one of these) and get him to find out everything he can about your intended before you make your move.

The other way, which works great in any cafe, especially a nice trendy one with sofas, is good for the weekends when people go there to chill out. Curl up with a book or the Sunday paper and enjoy your downtime for its own sake—but if you want to look up and around and strike up a chat with a handsome stranger, so much the better. Sexy bitches always have an excellent and intriguing book in their handbag. It goes without saying that reading everything you can get your hands on will make you a more interesting person and it's a bonus if the knowledge you acquire can then be used to spark a conversation that leads to a date. Even if he's not interested, he won't think, "There goes that girl who hit on me." He'll think, "There she is again: that mysterious brunette who knew so much about Dostoyevsky."

supermarkets

A single glance at a man's shopping basket can tell you about his relationship status. You're looking for meals for one, not Pampers. Supermarkets can be hugely busy and the manic energy levels mean it's easy to be really sassy. Steal something from his shopping basket or move your "next customer please" sign into his space accidentally on purpose so he'll have to accuse you of stealing his shopping. Don't rule out the out-of-town supermarket, either, as people tend to visit them on the same night every week and spend more time there, leaving you longer to cast your spell. Only problem is—he might be an out-of-towner, and no self-respecting sexy bitch wants to date a man whose distance from her own apartment has to be measured in hours rather than minutes.

parks

Parks have almost unlimited pick-up potential, whether you're trying to make eyes at a man from a nearby office who's enjoying his sandwich under an oak tree or just leering at the lycra-clad rollerbladers on a lazy Sunday afternoon. A lot of parks have men in their twenties playing a little casual football or frisbee after work or on the weekends. Find out where their game is and what days they play on and park yourself and a friend minxily in the center of the game, or have a little picnic in the goal. They'll have to take notice of you, if only to ask you to get out the way, and you can get a bit of flirting in then and keep the link by yelling at them while they play. They'll invariably go and replace lost fluids in a nearby bar and if you look impressed they might invite you along, too.

The second approach requires a dog. Dogs, like babies, transform you into a small-scale celebrity—if you've got a nice dog, complete strangers will come and start chatting to you about him/her. It's the most amazing icebreaker ever. Likewise, if a cute guy has a cute dog, it gives you license to talk to him. Start by asking the dog's name and from there move on to how long his walk is, where the dog and owner live and stuff. One golden rule—never, ever try and get off with a man who is walking a cat on a leash, for more reasons than there are pages in this book.

work

This is a good place to look for a long-term relationship, and nowhere more so than in the city, where there is a constant stream of new people and potential lovers every working day, from the people who share our buses to the other people who work in our office building to the horny little devil in the mailroom to the guy at the next desk. In fact, two thirds of city-dwellers meet their partners at work.

Any relationship that starts off in the office is bound to last for a number of reasons. You see each other as you really are when you work closely together. It's hard to put someone on a pedestal when you've seen him swearing at the photocopier and nursing a hangover under fluorescent lighting. Also, because there's every chance you're going to be seeing the other person whether you like it or not, people tend not to leap into office romances willy-nilly. By the same token, the office is not a great idea for a mad passionate fling—unless you can stand the ignominy of sharing office space with someone who knows what you look like naked. There are other pitfalls to office affairs, like sexual discrimination laws, for instance, and the embarrassment of rejection if you hit on a colleague who doesn't like you back. Office gossip can work for you as well as against you. If you don't have the chutzpah to let your crush know you like him, a word in the ear of the most indiscreet woman in the company might be quicker than actually telling him yourself.

The sooner you can find out if he's single, the less valuable man-hunting time you lose pining after someone who's already attached.

> **TIP**
>
> Which professions are best for meeting guys? Male-dominated environments like banking, technology and finance (think stuffy offices where everyone has to wear ties) are good; female-dominated professions like teaching and fashion aren't. As a general rule, the more people you meet in the course of your work, the more chances you have. So travel, PR, recruitment—all these will bring a weird and wonderful world of people onto your path. And, of course, a lot of them come with expense accounts. Which has nothing to do with dating. It's just fun.

Make sure you bump into him on Monday morning and ask what he did over the weekend. If he watched the game with the boys and went clubbing, chances are he's on the market and you may proceed. If he answers, "We went to Ikea," forget it. He's someone else's.

Huge corporations can be very anonymous and confusing. This works to your advantage because you can fool him into thinking he knows you. Just grin and ask how he is. You'll sow the seeds of curiosity in his mind and he'll spend so long wondering if you've worked together or if he's met you out and about that an image of you will drift in and out of his line of vision throughout his working day.

Organize a team-building trip to the local bowling alley and ask him to help get people on board. Not only is it a great, informal way to get to know all your colleagues, the element of competition will act as an aphrodisiac and fabulous you will disprove the theory that people who run work social committees are deeply tragic individuals like Patty from *Grease*.

traveling

The city commute is one of the less fabulous aspects of city life, but you'll be surprised how easy it is to turn the daily trek into a white-knuckle ride of sexual anticipation. Even the shortest commute is packed with opportunities to meet men (unless, of course, you work from home, in which case you'll be working the cafes and libraries circuit).

Most of us have a traveling-to-work routine that varies by about 30 seconds every day (mitigating factors include hangovers, not being able to find a clean, run-free pair of pantyhose and there being something really good about George Clooney coming up on the entertainment news right after these messages from our sponsors). And it's this seemingly dull, eventless, autopilot routine that is the key to man-hunting success.

Why? Well, if you spot a potential date just once, whether he's stopping off at the gas station or he's leaving the parking lot at the same time as you, you're way likelier to see him again. The thing about having a well-paid and responsible job (ah, shut up about creative fulfillment already—he needs to be able to keep you in *Cosmos* and Manolos, right?) is that it turns a man into a creature of routine.

He'll likely as not do the same little routine day in, day out, on his working week.

in the car

So you, sitting in your car, fixing your lipstick at the exact same time, at the exact same lights every morning, could be waiting right next to a guy who takes that same opportunity to straighten his tie. All it takes is for one of you to look around and lay eyes on the person you were put on this earth to love.

Now, you want to catch his attention without actually doing something the traffic cops could legitimately haul you in for, so your options are kind of limited. There isn't room for subtlety. The best tactic is to simply scrawl your cell phone number and the words "Call me" in lipstick on your window, although you might want to practice the necessary mirror-writing technique for this one. Try to lip-read when he's singing along. Is he crooning a Garth Brooks song or rapping along to P. Diddy? Figure it out, then tune your radio to a station that plays the tunes he loves. Turn it up loud and make sure your windows are open.

And while you're behind the wheel, take advantage of the fact that for once you have eyes in the back of your head and use your rear-view mirror to make eye contact with everyone from the sexy chauffeur in that Mercedes behind you to his equally sexy but probably richer male passenger, to the delivery boys on bikes to potential pedestrians.

on the train

In the big city, you're as likely to take—gasp!—public transport as you are to drive yourself into the office every day. Don't stick your cute little nose up at the idea of taking the subway or a bus to get to work because you'll be missing out on a bevy of pick-up possibilities.

So let's say you take the subway or the El. Ever noticed how seasoned commuters know exactly which spot to stand on so they're aligned with their favorite door of their favorite carriage when the train pulls into the station? Simply find out your victim's—sorry, I mean the object of your desire's—little standing space. Use the pigeon shit and chewing gum inevitably stuck to the concrete to get your bearings if need be, and then one day, get there a day or so early and stand there. Right on his spot. If he's a creature of habit (and aren't they all?), he'll be so thrown by this minute change in his morning routine that his mind, body and soul will be awakened and tuned into the possibility of new and exciting things happening today. A sassy smile acknowledging that your behavior is deliberate will only enhance your chances.

Once you're on the train, try to sit opposite him rather than next to him. No one makes eye contact with the person sitting next to them. (Save sitting next to boys you like for the journey home, when he might be tired and fall asleep on your shoulder.)

A newspaper is a must, and the wider you spread it the better. Hold a tabloid open so he can see today's scandalous headlines as well as the sports page, then suddenly lower it—his eyes will have been transfixed to that spot and when the paper's taken away, he'll be left gazing into your eyes. Newspapers (or classy magazines, or intellectual-looking books) are also great for hiding behind and looking up coyly from.

on the bus

Then there's the bus. Look up the phrase "cheap thrills" in the dictionary and there should be a picture of a rush-hour bus right there. For less than the price of a tall latte at Starbucks, you can get to work and cop a feel of any guy who strikes your fancy. Simply squeeze onto the standing-room-only bus during rush hour, getting as near to your boyfriend-to-be as you decently (or indecently) can. It goes without saying that if you're strap-hanging, underarm hygiene has to be high on your list of priorities. Wait until the bus rounds a corner and then let centrifugal force be your guide; swing your whole body around so it's millimeters away from his. You'll find that nearly touching him is a far better turn-on than pressing your body so tightly against him that the lace from your Wonderbra leaves a little imprint on the skin on his chest. Girls aren't the only ones who can feel like their personal space is being invaded, and less is, in this case, more, more, more.

in a cab

In the movies, people are always meeting in cabs—strangers share cabs and end up falling in love, you know the score. In real life, a) I've never heard of this actually happening, and b) I think it's pretty dangerous to jump into a cab with a guy you've never met and let him see where you live before you've even talked about how you're going to split the fare. My advice? Quit taking cabs into work every day unless you want to end up a) with a stalker, or b) dating some random immigrant taxi driver who always smells of car freshener and gasoline. Get out on the street, take the bus and use all that money you were spending on cabs to dress yourself in Victoria's Secret's finest.

And finally: don't like the guys you see every day? Vary your routine by leaving for work half an hour early. It's a brand new world of passionate possibilities out there, *and* you get to impress your boss and male co-workers, too.

places where there are loads of men

Go where statistics are on your side and the absence of any other attractive females makes it more likely that you'll stand out and the men will be more desperate, ahem, I mean eager for female company. While you could hang around an oil rig in Alaska, where there are something like 150 men for every woman, I've had a look around and there are no branches of Karen Millen in the middle of the North Sea, so that won't do. And agricultural fairs are seething with men, but the chances of your sexy bitch fabulous urban lifestyle being compatible with pitchforks and cow-milking are so slim as to make them not worth your while.

The key to finding large groups of men is "special interest." I'm talking cult TV, music, motors. Sociologists have found that while women tend to meet up with their friends for the sake of it, just to talk, and their choice of venue is secondary, men spend time with their friends because they want someone to share their activities with. Men place much more importance than women on finding a partner who shares their taste.

Now, I'm not for one second saying that you should fake an interest in something that you don't care for at all—you'll come across as fake and, frankly, a little crazy. I'm just saying that next time something sparks your interest in a magazine, take it a bit further, do some research on the internet, find out where the live events are, and buy a ticket.

music

Is music the food of love? It's certainly a serious weapon in the armory of the urban dater. It's never been researched, but I'm willing to bet that if you cross-sectioned a man's brain and a woman's brain, there would be a small segment of male brain shaped like a filing cabinet with every tune he's ever heard filed neatly in alphabetical order.

Maybe this takes up the bit of brain that would otherwise be preoccupied with commitment. I don't know. All I'm saying is it's very rare to find a man who isn't, to some extent, a bit of a music snob. For this reason, any woman who is remotely passionate about music should exploit this fact to the fullest. Record shops are great places to pretend to be browsing. The used and rarities section is a godsend because when the man you've got your eye on picks up a rare Jimi Hendrix vinyl, you can dash over to him and pretend you were just about to get it yourself. Make a smart comment about how Prince would never have become the living legend he is without *Are You Experienced*. For further research, rent *High Fidelity* and imagine what you would do to seduce John Cusack's character. *High Fidelity* is also worth watching because Jack Black's character is a prime example of straddling the fine line between cool and geeky music fan and just plain geeky and weird music freak. You're looking for a guy who thinks that all the songs are written about you—not someone who thinks women are just a nuisance who eat into his valuable listening/chin stroking/masturbating time. Rock concerts are great because club rules apply (i.e., dark, drunk, dancing)—plus the men in the audience will be so charged with adrenaline and testosterone at the spectacle of their favorite band they'll be deluded that they too are rock gods and are ripe for flattering pick-up lines that indulge this fantasy. Dress a bit like a groupie by doing something messy with your hair and showing lots of flesh.

stars

When men get into sci-fi, something weird happens—they obsess and can become overly excited by anything, anything that is even remotely connected with "Star Trek," *Stargate, Alien* or whatever space odyssey it is that lights his personal touchpad. It therefore stands to reason that any woman seen in an environment that is primarily dominated by sci-fi ephemera will by default become twice as sexy and attractive as she actually is. Normal social boundaries don't exist here: It's perfectly acceptable to march up to strange men and ask them their opinion on any vaguely related subject. After all, in "Star Trek Voyager," the ship is captained by a woman. However, if he can only get aroused if you dress up as a Klingon and shout "Beam me up, Scotty" at the moment of orgasm, you've obviously got a problem, but otherwise you should be fine. If you really can't bear sci-fi, substitute the *Lord of the Rings* trilogy. Although it's technically fantasy, not science fiction, it appeals to the same demographic. Try tucking your hair behind your ears à la Liv Tyler as Arwen and watch the guys flock to you. These boys tend to be shy and will love it that you are so feisty and up front.

cars

Don't ask me why going fast is a man thing, but it is. Men and motors also go together like girls and make-up: Check out automobile magazines for news of car shows. Rent a sports car or drape yourself across the hood (bikini optional) while checking out a new model. Call her "she," or play dumb and give him the chance to talk about his favorite thing.

2 urban male types

For the sexy bitch, who doesn't like to compromise her fabulous social life, her career, her friends or anything else for the sake of a guy, mismatched lifestyles can smother the most promising liaisons quicker than any other factor, including lack of sexual chemistry or long distances. I've lost count of the number of times my flaky, arty bohemian friends have fallen out with their new banker boyfriends, or my construction worker pals have been bewildered by the power-suited career girls they've dated.

While lifestyle compatibility is more important in the city than anywhere else, nowhere is it harder to achieve. For example, if you both come from a small fishing village, chances are you'll have your local pub and a healthy interest in the shipping forecast in common. A random encounter with one of the millions of men who live in your city, however, doesn't guarantee any shared interests.

To improve the odds of meeting a man whose lifestyle matches your own, you need to know what kind of men you can choose from. Here are the most common and easily identifiable breeds of the urban male species. This information will allow you to locate and recognize him. It also predicts the kind of boyfriend he'll make so you can eliminate him from your dating game if he's going to be unsuitable.

There's also some advice on how to seduce him because the fact a man was unsuitable never stopped any of us in the past....

mr. mama's boy

A man over 18 who still lived at home with his parents used to be a bit of a loser, but don't dismiss a stay-at-home boy too quickly. The crazy escalation in house prices means that shrewd young urban professionals are now going home to roost rent-free and save enough money for a deposit on a huge bachelor pad with a view of the river.

FIND HIM: Playing basketball with the guys or propping up the bar, safe in the knowledge that Mom will cook his dinner and do his laundry when he gets home. Because he's desperate to get out of the house the whole time, he has an excellent social life (and is amenable to mini-breaks much earlier on in the relationship than his condo-owning counterparts).

SEDUCE HIM BY: Mentioning you've got your own place and you can cook—oh, and you're an easy lay. That'll give him the creature comforts of mom's house with one creature comfort she certainly doesn't provide him. You hope.

LONG-TERM LOVING: As a boyfriend, Mr. Mama's Boy is loyal and loving, but he might expect you to do everything for him. After all, that's what he's used to. His lack of privacy at home might mean he "unofficially" moves in with you for weeks on end. Your roommates, if you have them, might not think this is as cute as you do. If you still live with your parents, too, you'd better forget it unless you both have a kinky streak and get off on the idea of sex in public places. It might be sexy in a teenagers-in-love way for the first couple of weeks, but after a while it'll drive you crazy. It's not all bad news, though. Get on the right side of his mom and you could find a couple of nights a week you don't have to cook, either.

mr. tourist

Every big U.S. city has an area—usually near the train station—where the young European guys hang out. I'm talking travelers, tourists, backpackers—call 'em what you will. All that matters to the sexy bitch is that he's hot, horny, thousands of miles away from home and all too keen to seek comfort in the arms of a sexy stranger—and that's where you come in. Just make sure you know the word "condom" in his language and embark on a no-strings fling (and if you part on good terms, potentially a free bed next time you're in the mood for an exotic vacation).

FIND HIM: Hanging out at the most obvious nightspot in town, or mooching around the usual traps—Beale Street in Memphis, outside Manns Chinese Theater in L.A., the Met in New York—pretty much anywhere you think you're too cool to hang out because it's full of idiot tourists. There will always be one strategically placed bar or coffee shop where all the tourists congregate together (which defeats the purpose of trying to experience a new culture for them, but means less effort for you). Rather sadly and predictably, they'll often gravitate towards McDonald's, KFC or some other global brand just to get a fix of what they're already familiar with, so swallow your pride and see who you can make eye contact with over a McFlurry. Most people abandon their sexual mores on vacation—they're open to new experiences, whether it's learning a language or learning what the Great American Sexy Bitch is like in bed.

SEDUCE HIM BY: Plopping yourself, all dolled up, in a sea of British, Australian, French or Greek guys— your novelty value alone will get you extra interest from them. Overexaggerate your local accent. They will find it charming. And if he's British or Australian, you don't even need to have anything in common—you can sustain a two-hour conversation just getting each other to repeat words like "coffee" and marveling at how differently you pronounce them.

LONG-TERM LOVING: There isn't any, really, which is great because it means you can get down and dirty and enjoy yourself without worrying about the consequences. Ironically, this is often when we totally let our guards down and find it easy to be ourselves and fall in love. Just be careful of falling madly in love and take any promises of carrying on a relationship with a pinch of salt. Oh, and if you hear the words "Green Card" at any time, run. Like the wind.

mr. city slicker

He works hard, plays hard, and his suits are so sharp his secretary could use them to open his mail. He'll have his own apartment with all mod cons that he often shares with a roommate because he wants to have bachelor fun rather than to save money. This guy earns a fortune and doesn't care who knows it, which is handy for the sexy bitch, who prides herself on being the kind of independent woman who doesn't mind someone else picking up the bar tab.

FIND HIM: Somewhere expensive and exclusive—dress code is good, members-only even better. City slickers don't tend to socialize too far from their offices just in case they have to rush back and broker an important deal at a moment's notice. An increasing number of large corporations have their own unofficial bar like in "Ally McBeal" (although if you ask me, they spent *way* too much time all hanging out in that piano bar. No wonder they were taken off the air). So if it's an investment banker you're after, look up some investment banking firms and ask the receptionist, switchboard operator or security guard where the great and the good of the company go to drink. Make this place your regular haunt—every hunter observes her prey in its natural environment before working out the best method of capture.

SEDUCE HIM BY: Asking him about work. Catch him when his defenses are down and his liver is pickled at the end of the night by offering to share his cab. If you're lucky enough to pick up a city slicker with his own driver, this line works even better.

LONG-TERM LOVING: He never switches off, so if he's not unwinding in a bar, he's venting his frustrations on the weights at the gym and might not be up for cozy nights on the sofa in front of the Comedy Channel. If your own career is high-octane, beware of competition: You're both used to being the best, and this might make compromise tricky. You'll compete over everything from who earns the most to who's most stressed at the end of the working week.

mr. hipster

He's the guy with just-got-out-of-bed hair that took him three hours to perfect. Perhaps the most urban of all urban men, he would probably go into a tailspin if he had to leave the city center. Since he hasn't been out of the city except to go to another one in the last few years, that's not a problem. He shivers when he hears the word "suburbs" (probably because he grew up in one and is desperately trying to escape).

FIND HIM: In the newest, trendiest bars, clubs and galleries in town. When I say new and trendy, I mean new and trendy. If the bar or club has already been written-up in any mainstream newspaper or magazine, it's too popular and he can't be seen there. He likes to be wherever there are models or art students, preferably both: the models satisfy his high aesthetic standards, while the art students stimulate his creative side.

SEDUCE HIM BY: Offering to buy him a bottle of an obscure Japanese beer that's limited edition, letting the label on your top show (this, of course, only works if it's designer or vintage—Banana Republic isn't a name to have any man, let alone this dedicated follower of fashion, slavering at your feet). Asking him if he was the DJ who was profiled in this month's *W* magazine.

LONG-TERM LOVING: He's got such high standards you'll feel special that he's chosen you, and it's important that his woman looks nice so he'll take you shopping. On the other hand, he's a nightmare because you can never keep up with this guy unless you're a fashionista yourself, in which case, start planning your wedding now. Slobby weekends in tracksuits are out.

mr. football

By football, I, of course, also mean baseball, basketball, racing, soccer or whatever sport lights this guy's candle. If you're lucky, he'll make himself known to you by wearing a cap or shirt with his team logo so you'll know what you're dealing with from the outset. He tends to travel in a pack—his social life revolves around his sport-loving buddies.

FIND HIM: In a sports bar that's televising the game.

SEDUCE HIM BY: Wearing his team shirt and hinting that you've got panties to match. Don't make the mistake of actually trying to chat him up during the game—you could dance naked wearing nothing but nipple tassles in his team colors and it wouldn't make a bit of difference. If you must try and insinuate yourself while he's playing, rush over and hug him whenever his team scores. For some reason, the normal rules don't apply here—men who think even shaking hands is a tad gay will happily give their pals full body hugs. Take advantage of this.

LONG-TERM LOVING: Great because when it develops into a real relationship, you won't have him around getting in the way of shopping and facials and all the other things you would normally have to do on a Saturday if you were single, so in a way it's the best of both worlds. Unless—heaven forbid—he always wants the boys over to watch the game, in which case you'll be washing the smell of beer, cigarettes and potato chips out of your hair all week, only for it to start again on Monday. Because his friends are such an important part of his life, if all goes wrong, you can always move on to them. And if all goes right, you've got a captive cluster of eligible bachelors to introduce your single friends to.

mr. commitment

No, that's not a printing error—there is a growing breed of young single men out there hungry for love. Great if you've had your share of the bad bastards, but remember, a man over 35 who's willing to share his sperm and hasn't found anyone to do so with is probably single for a reason

FIND HIM: Hanging around with his couple friends (to help him learn about how relationships work), hanging around with his single friends (to increase the chances of ending up in a club and taking someone home), hanging around with his female friends (partly with the hope that they'll tell him where he's going wrong, partly because he hopes they might fall in love with him if only they spend enough time with him)…you get the picture.

SEDUCE HIM BY: Not holding your stomach in so he gets an idea of what you'd look like pregnant. Raising the subject of the future and making it clear you're looking to settle down, too.

LONG-TERM LOVING: If you're sure you want the real deal and babies and stuff, then by all means give this guy a go, but don't rush into anything. He might be *sooo* deafened by the ticking of his biological clock that he can't hear anything you say and doesn't get to know the real you until three weeks before the wedding, when it dawns on him you're not really that compatible after all. Rushing into his arms for the wrong reasons might leave you feeling stifled and longing for the old days of nights out with the girls or alone with a family-size pizza and *Steel Magnolias* on TV.

mr. rough

Think "Joe Millionaire": he's an old-fashioned, hard-working, blue-collar gentleman who won't let the lady pay for anything—and he earns a lot more than his battered clothes suggest. His job involves a lot of time outside, whether it's standing at a market stall or climbing up scaffolding at a construction site.

FIND HIM: At work—remember, these boys don't keep nine-to-five hours and are often up at the crack of dawn. Often they're eating their breakfast in the park while you're on your way to work, so make the most of these magic few hours in the day (when your make-up has yet to melt off your face) by walking past him, looking stunning every morning.

SEDUCE HIM BY: Buying just one single cucumber every morning from his market stall. Whistle back when he whistles at you.

LONG-TERM LOVING: He'll always be good at lifting things and killing spiders, and will leave many major purchase decisions up to you but will occasionally supply the cash. He's more likely to let you choose his clothes than any of the other urban male breeds. Sex will be great and for once you won't mind doing it in missionary because he'll have an upper body that's worth looking at from such close range. He'll make you feel vulnerable, girly and looked after, and you'll astonish yourself by enjoying it. Over time, the novelty of your blue-collar boyfriend might wear off: when he wears his paint-splattered jeans to your company's black-tie Christmas ball, for example. *However,* he could well live in the suburbs and only go where the jobs are. Just because he hangs out in the big city doesn't mean it's his idea of fun after-hours.

mr. caring sharing

So in touch with his feminine side he has period cramps. He's a social worker or teacher, totally at odds with other city boys who are concerned with success, image, and money. He's more likely to spend his last $20 renewing his subscription to *Yoga Journal* than on your cabfare home at the end of the night—but he'll always offer to give you a ride home on the handle of his bicycle.

FIND HIM: At a demonstration protesting something, whether it's the situation in the Middle East or animal testing, or shopping in your local organic, cruelty-free, vegan store.

SEDUCE HIM BY: Asking him to sign your petition, or if he knows the best way to patch your flat bicycle tire.

LONG-TERM LOVING: Make sure you take him out of the city before you commit to him because he might not be as caring as he seems. A lot of urban eco warriors drone on about saving the planet from their lovely heated condo in the middle of town but change their minds about the evils of the modern world when they find themselves stuck in marshland in the middle of nowhere, miles from the nearest pesticide-free tomato. If he's genuine, know that a relationship with him means living by his rules—expect lectures on how much energy is wasted on packaging cosmetics every time you come home with a new Clinique lipstick. Oh, and he'll be into equal rights so that means you'll have to go on top sometimes.

mr. clubber

You'll be seduced into his wildly exciting nighttime world of drink, drugs, dancing and decadence. He'll be funny and popular, and he'll never judge you for getting too drunk, mainly because he's always stoned, too, and is never sober for long enough to pass judgment on anything apart from where the next party is.

FIND HIM: By checking the nightlife section of the *L.A. Weekly* (or your local equivalent) for where the serious clubbers are going this weekend; or hanging around on street corners waiting for a man named Raver to turn up with Saturday night's drugs.

SEDUCE HIM BY: Mopping his brow and getting him a glass of water; giving him a back rub and talking about his vinyl collection in the chill-out room. This shows off your nurturing side as well as proves you're in with club culture.

LONG-TERM LOVING: Over time, you'll need to think about whether you can handle being with a man who spends most of his time out of his head in hot, sweaty rooms full of scantily clad women. And when the party's over, he'll want his woman to pick up the pieces. The sex won't be great unless Viagra is his recreational drug of choice. Party drugs (booze, dope) tend to make a guy lose his erection completely, or give him a never-ending boner (Ecstasy, coke), which isn't as much fun as it sounds at four o'clock in the morning when you're counting the cracks in the ceiling and have been for the last 45 minutes.

mr. lothario

He could do anything for a living and his looks are unpredictable, but he does need to live in the city because that's the only place where there are enough woman to satisfy this 21st-century Casanova's lust for, well, lust. Often, he genuinely believes that he's a real catch and it's only fair to give every woman he meets the opportunity to sleep with him. If only this guy would wear a T-shirt saying "heartbreaker," life would be so much easier.

FIND HIM: Everywhere—you'll recognize him by his charm and confidence rather than any other outward signals. You'll know it's him when he can undo your bra strap in 0.1 seconds. With one hand. In the dark.

SEDUCE HIM BY: Honey, you won't get a chance to think about seduction because he'll get in there first and you won't know what's hit you.

LONG-TERM LOVING: You'll think you can tame him. So did all the others. Instead, the best you can do is warn all your girlfriends about him, thank him for the interesting things he taught you in bed (because he will know exactly what he's doing in that department) and start looking for someone worthy of your new bedroom skills.

3 entrapment

So you know who you're looking for and where to find him. All you need to do now is make him yours. As a sexy bitch, you're able to carry off the corniest lines (example: "Do you believe in love at first sight or shall I walk past you again?"), but that's almost too easy—you're looking for a seduction technique that oozes class and sophistication but also definitely has an undercurrent of sluttiness.

Some guys can handle women marching right on up and announcing their sexual intentions. But your average guy will respond to a direct proposition with abject terror. While we wait for the majority of guykind to catch up with the enlightened few who can handle a sexy bitch's go-get-him attitude, we need to use cunning to make him think he's come onto you.

Use words that invite him to pursue you further rather than being blatant about what you want. "Don't I know you from somewhere?" is a tried-and-true line that saves face if he blanks you with a "No," but can lead to conversations where you swap details of your friends, jobs and backgrounds as you try to establish something (other than sexual chemistry) that you might have in common.

Sharing any kind of experience can be a great shortcut to intimacy—for example, you might want to take the fact you were both at the same Prince concert in 1990 as a million-to-one coincidence and a sign that you should be together forever, but you better go home and

"

have sex right now just to check you're physically as well as musically compatible.

Once you've caught his name, use it. Don't be afraid to compliment him on how heartbreakingly good-looking he is. Trust me, he'll translate "That shirt really looks good on you"as a declaration of his status as an urban Adonis.

Establish his status as early as you can to avoid disappointment and embarrassment on both your accounts. There's nothing more disheartening than wasting a couple of hours chatting to somebody else's guy, and nothing more awkward than the moment when he tells you he's taken. Ironically, the men in long-term relationships are often the easiest to start talking to because a) they're more secure and therefore easy-going than single guys out on the prowl, and b) they often enjoy a little innocent flirtation and banter for its own sake and find it hard to resist the ego-boost of having a beautiful woman pay them a little bit of attention.

Annoyingly, it's not always obvious when a man's in a committed relationship and therefore off limits. There are some outward signs: he's wearing a wedding band, for example, or has that pale imprint on his third finger, left hand, that makes you wonder why he isn't wearing his ring.

If possible, ask other people about your target first. A simple "Who's he?" will often prompt mutual acquaintances to tell you if he's taken. If you don't know anyone in common, just be playful and ask, "Where's your girlfriend tonight then?" It's a bit tacky, but you're flattering him by assuming that a hot stud like him will already be taken and subtly making it clear that you have a vested interest in whether or not he's single.

how a sexy bitch's girlfriends can help—and hinder—her dating prowess

Any sexy bitch worth her Tiffany pendant should make a point having remarkable friends, but any SB who wants a boyfriend to buy her a matching bracelet should think long and hard when choosing which friends she goes man-hunting with.

Friends can be hugely important when it comes to meeting men. For a starters, surrounding yourself with wonderful people who love you will boost your confidence like nothing else can. And you're never more likely to meet that special guy than when you're not looking for him. If the aim of your night is to catch up on gossip, dance yourself dizzy, drink lots of Cosmopolitans and laugh until cranberry juice comes out of your nose, then a kiss will be an unexpected bonus.

But the wrong friends can hinder, rather than help, your chances of meeting someone. It's important to realize that just because someone is a great co-worker / shopping partner / boozing buddy it doesn't necessarily follow that they'll be a good pick-up partner.

Sometimes it's obvious. When I've been to straight clubs with gay friends, I've often come home pissed that the guy who caught my eye hasn't so much as returned a smile. With hindsight, it's blindingly apparent that few men are going to want to approach a woman who, when she's not making up moves to "Vogue" on the dance floor, is deep in conversation with or even hugging a variety of very good-looking twenty-something boys. And the ones who do are probably trying to get off with said boys rather than you. Sometimes it's more subtle. For example, you'd think my friend Michelle would be my perfect pick-up partner because she's gorgeous, gregarious and likes the same pubs and clubs as me. But our man missions have always ended in failure simply because we're too busy enjoying each other's company to pay attention to any men who might be checking us out.

Often, our friends keep us in our comfort zone. When you're a singleton and all your friends seem to be attached, it's all too easy to spend your Saturday nights having dinner with them because it's safe and cozy. But unless the male half of the couple provides you with a different potential partner each time you meet, you're never going to find a guy to make your toes tingle in that Thai restaurant you've eaten at five Saturdays in succession.

The right pick-up partner is as hard to find as a decent man but, like falling in love, when you find her, you'll just know. She'll have the same agenda as you and will understand that it's necessary to have a pre-pick-up plan of action because the only thing worse than standing aimlessly like a lemon while your friend tries to get off with some beautiful creature is having her stand around while you're trying to get off with one. Establish a code word or phrase (something subtle such as "Anyone for tequila slammers?") that you'll use when it's time for one of you to at least disappear to the bathroom for five minute to give the other time to get her claws into her prey. If there's a bar with a balcony, so much the better. You can lean over it on your own without looking like you're on the prowl, enjoy the view and sooner or later someone will come and talk to you. Never fails.

dress to impress

Sadly, there's no such thing as an outfit that will have men falling at your feet (can you imagine the crush in the Saks changing rooms if there were?). But you can do a couple of things to increase your chances.

Flashing flesh will attract a lot of male attention, but too much cleavage or leg on display and you might—I'm sorry to have to tell you—attract the kind of guy who only wants you for your body (which isn't always a good thing). Wear something you feel confident in. A couple of my male friends say they like to see girls in powder pink or baby blue, but if your trusty little black dress gives you kick-ass confidence, then stick with it. If it fits and flatters you, then you'll be wearing it, rather than it wearing you.

Don't be a fashion victim. Your girlfriends might *ooh* and *aah* and understand exactly how your look is working when you team your Prada stilettos with your Issey Miyake puffball trousers and top it all off with an "ironic" necklace made out of Sweet Tarts that was an absolute steal at Wet Seal. Men will just think you look like an escapee from the psychiatric hospital—the chances of him having seen pictures of the latest catwalk collections are slimmer than a supermodel on a diet.

Likewise, keep make-up glamorous rather than avant-garde. If you're in a low-lighting situation, feel free to have fun with smoky eyes and pouty lips, but don't experiment with fluorescent yellow mascara. If it doesn't make you look prettier, leave it in your make-up bag. Hair should be clean, shiny and, above all, *touchable*. Luckily, our generation will never be victim to solid, helmet-like, First Lady hairdos, but it's still possible to overdo it with the product. If it doesn't move when you shake your head, how is he going to be able to run his fingers through it?

Perfume-wise, men like vanilla-based or musky smells because they remind them of eating and screwing, respectively. So leave your florals and citrussy smells at home and appeal to his more basic instincts.

body language

Body language is the oldest form of communication. Cavepeople, with their vocabulary of three different kinds of grunts, didn't have the language to communicate who they liked, but instead instinctively interpreted subtleties like posture and facial expression to play out a primitive version of the dating game.

It still comes in very handy today. A flick of the hair or a strategically placed leg can say "I want you, big boy" in a subtle, subconscious way that words will never be able to. Physical flirting is where accessories really come into their own. Everything from a cocktail stick to a stiletto shoe is a potential prop in your seduction routine. You'll find that you do a lot of these things already without being aware of it when you're trying to impress a guy you like, but it won't hurt to execute your movements with that extra little bit of finesse.

None of the following will work if you don't start out with the right eye contact. If you're nervous and full-on eye contact seems to be asking a lot, look from eye to eye or even the inner corners of his ears. If he's more than a couple of feet away, he won't know the difference. Don't stare him down unsmilingly as that will just make you look like you're recovering from laser eye surgery and can't quite focus again yet. Instead, once you've caught his eye, hold his gaze for a second or two and then look down bashfully and coyly. I appreciate bashful and coy might not come easy to you, but the aim of the game is to entice him over to you rather than give him the same beady eye an eagle would her prey. After a minute or so, glance in his direction again. If he's looking at you, smile and look away again. If he returns your smile, the scene is set for a little more flirtation.

Dangle your shoe off the end of your foot. The higher the heel, the longer and shapelier it'll make your leg look. The beauty of this move is that it looks as sexy as hell but if you do it nonchalantly enough, it won't look at all deliberate, and absent-minded sluttishness beats contrived sluttishness hands down every time. If you're feeling minxish and he's within reach, you can actually slip right out of the shoe and rub your feet up and down his calf.

Caress your collarbone in the direction of your cleavage—you can bet his eyes will keep wandering down even if your fingers don't. Let your bra strap show. Women will tut at you but men find this incredibly, teasingly sexy. Well, the ones I know do, anyway.

Brush past his butt. It's very suggestive but you can always pretend it was an accident. Use the back of your hand to caress just under his waistband at the back. This one only really works in traditional pick-up joints where flirting is on the menu, and the more crowded the venue, the more he'll wonder if you really meant it or not. Avoid doing this in deserted parks or office corridors.

Make sure your whole torso is facing him full-on. Just as a sunflower grows toward the sun, so we instinctively face people we're attracted to.

Look him up and down slowly, without focusing on individual body parts—just as you hate it when he stares at your tits, he won't thank you for gawking at his fly. Wink at him. This sends out strong signals, but it's just between the two of you so no one else is going to know about it if he returns your wink with a stony stare.

Touching yourself invites your partner to do the same. Lightly stroke your own collarbone or outer thigh. Showing the inside skin like wrists, armpits or inner thighs, body language experts say, signifies vulnerability, and if you want to show a man you like him by adopting a legs-akimbo, hands-in-the-air pose, that's fine by me. But I would rather you stroked the soft skin on the inside of your arm.

If you're nervous, it's tempting to go crazy and play with your hair. I have long hair that I'm constantly twizzling around my fingers; I've done it on dates, at job interviews, even on TV once, and people are constantly telling me it makes me look like an insane witch. I get around it by wearing a ring and twizzling that instead.

Change your body language and see if he mirrors it. When we like someone, we unknowingly mimic their posture. Keep it subtle, though—start Vogueing and you'll just look crazy and that will undo all your good work. Keep your movements small. Try re-crossing your legs in the opposite direction, or tilting your head to one side.

TIP

Some men think it's sexy when women apply lipstick in public. Personally, I think it looks like your mom didn't teach you any better, and it defeats the purpose if you're going for the no make-up make-up look. If you want to draw attention to your mouth (and you do, because that will get him thinking how much he'd like to kiss you), smile!

If he's someone you've met through friends, make your goodbye kiss on the cheek last a fraction of a second longer than it needs to. He'll notice, but no one else will so if he doesn't respond to this tiny sexual signal, you're the only two who'll know about it. It's safe but effective.

how to read *his* body language

So you're making all the right moves to seduce him but you need to know if it's working. These are the subtle body language signs he won't even know he's giving out to let you know whether he's interested in you or not.

Again, eyes are the windows of the soul, and eye contact is your easiest indicator. If he returns your stare for more than a couple of seconds, keep doin' watch yo' doin', sister. If he's looking over your shoulder at other girls, or at the floor, it means he doesn't want to talk to you. If he's looking down but manages to raise his eyes to yours for split seconds at a time, chances are he's just shy so be gentle with the delicate little flower.

If he leans forward and rests his chin on his hand, he's interested. His hand should be lightly touching his face, not supporting a bored, drooping jaw. If he actually has to hold up his own head, you're doing something wrong.

If he crosses his arms and legs, making a shield for you, or puts his hands in his pockets, that's a bad sign—he's putting up a barrier between you.

Watch his smile. If his eyes crinkle, it's genuine. If the eyes are dead even when the lips are moving, then it's not—move on. He's humoring you, which shows that he's too polite to tell you he's not up for it.

He'd be mortified if he knew he was doing it, but if he wants to take things further, he'll absent-mindedly stroke his hair, his beard (or stubble) and massage the hair around his temples. If he raises his eyebrows, he's interested.

You're in there if he brushes against you or picks imaginary bits of fluff off your top. This is part ancient grooming ritual that goes back to caveman days, part excuse to give your breasts a quick feel.

You know that thing they do when they sit down, knees wide apart? It looks as though they're trying to take up as much room as possible, and that's not far off—they want you to see how big and important and manly they are.

dirty tricks to make him yours

If you're not in a traditional pick-up joint, some of these strategies might be a little too subtle. If he sees you stroking your collarbone on the bus, for example, he'll certainly notice you, but he might not think it appropriate to approach you. So you need to work a bit harder by engineering situations that will bring you closer together.

Some of the happiest couples I know were thrown together by the unlikeliest of situations—a series of random events that could only be coincidence led to their meeting. Or at least that's what the women who carefully orchestrated the circumstances let their boyfriends believe.

It's very hard to simply strike up a conversation with a man outside of a traditional pick-up joint. The truth is, sometimes you need to subtly manipulate a situation or tell a little white lie to facilitate a conversation with your target.

If any of these techniques seem a bit contrived and fake, you're right. A lot of the things I'm asking you to try won't come naturally to you. But then, neither does your Rouge Noir manicure or your Wonderbra'd cleavage, and you don't feel guilty about using them to entrap men, do you? These strategies are simply ideas you can use to get yourself noticed and once they've worked their magic, it's up to your personality to do the bewitching.

Before you approach him, check out his mood. Timing is everything, so make sure he's relaxed and smiling. Men who are deep in conversation/shouting into cell phones/crying are unlikely to respond well to your advances. Don't even think about approaching him without having made eye contact and had a smile returned.

Do a couple of circuits of the venue, whether it's going up and down the frozen vegetables aisle twice in the supermarket or taking twice as long to walk back from the bathroom in the dentist's waiting room. This works twofold: You get to check out the entire range of manhood on offer, and you get to Be Seen. Walk tall and smile, so when you do approach him, you're a familiar image.

Make him feel useful. Ask him to light your cigarette, but only if you've noticed he's a smoker as well. Lock your keys in your car and feign girly helplessness. His willingness to help is also an indicator of how nice a guy he is. If he won't play knight in shining armor to a damsel in distress, he's not the kind of man you want to get to know anyway, no matter how nice his muscles are.

Ask for directions in the street and get him to point you in a destination that's towards where he's already walking. That makes it easy for you to fall into step with him and engineer a conversation.

When you do get chatting, speaking quietly makes him lean a little further in towards you and is a great shortcut to intimacy. What do you mean it's cheating? That's the whole point!

Lock your keys in your car and ask him to help you get them out. As a rule, the more sensible and law-abiding a man is, the more flattered he'll be that you thought he was the kind of untamable rogue that knew how to break into a car.

In an internet cafe, pretend you can't locate a certain key or are having problems with downloading or printing something. Have a website on screen that's a good conversation starter—a last-minute bargain vacations website, for example, will let him know you're a spontaneous, fun-loving chick who's just looking for someone to drive off into the sunset with.

Drop something in front of him. If he's a nice guy, he'll help you pick it up. I recommend dropping something fabulous, such as a shopping bag overflowing with Agent Provocateur underwear in a variety of colors and fabrics, to really get his attention.

Revolving doors offer excellent, if slightly surreal, flirtation opportunities. They're especially useful if you're going for the slow burn—i.e., gradually making yourself known to a man you see on a regular basis—rather than a sudden impact. Jump into the section of the door behind him and, just as he's about to walk out, accidentally-on-purpose push the door forward at top speed so he has to go all the way around again. He'll inevitably look around for the culprit, and his eyes will alight on your irresistibly smiling face.

Spill your drink all over him. Granted, this one could go either way, and it's best attempted with water, but at the very worst, it offers you the opportunity to dab at his manly chest with a napkin that might just have your phone number written on it. If you are going to go for this kind of grand gesture, make sure you have the confidence and sass to carry it off, otherwise it just won't work. A few years ago, I was on the tube on my way to work when a guy thrust a business card into my hand with "Call me—Lloyd" written on it. But when I looked up to see whose doing this was, he blushed scarlet, wouldn't meet my eyes and jumped off the train. Not exactly James Bond in terms of smoothness with the ladies—and it really put me off.

The more you practice these techniques, the more your attitude will change, until you're able to look for the man-meeting potential in any and every situation. My friend Lucy is a mistress of this particular art. She calls it "The Spirit of the Blitz" technique. Whenever there's any subject that has the whole country talking, she manages to turn it to her advantage, whether it's the Super bowl, a reality TV show or a big election. In 2000, we had a severe gasoline shortage in England. The whole country came to a standstill. It was terribly dramatic. Lucy, the sexy bitch that she is, managed to turn this time of national crisis to her dating advantage. While she was waiting to pay for a magazine in a gas station mini-mart, a rather handsome young man in front of her turned around and said, "It's really stressful, isn't it? How much gas do you have left?" Quick as a flash, she replied, "I'm down to half a tank." Cue a five-minute discussion about how stressful the gas crisis was and how it stopped you from taking life for granted, etc. They clicked so well they got coffee at a nearby cafe, and it wasn't until about half an hour into their conversation that Lucy confessed that not only did she not own a car, she didn't have so much as a driver's license—she'd just wanted an excuse to keep talking. He found this incredibly charming and, although romance never blossomed, they're now firm friends.

Gillian, a girl I used to work with, has convinced a guy who takes the same train as her every morning that they've known each other for years just by asking him how he is and, during their regular 20-minute chats on the journey into town, dropping in shared cultural references to things that happened ages ago—corny records they both bought when they were 12, or cult children's TV shows. He has yet to actually ask her where they met, but will often ask her if she remembers parties she wasn't even at. Be careful when you're employing this tactic not to actually create false memories—e.g., pretend you were at school together when he's from Cleveland and you're from Detroit—as you'll inevitably be found out and this is the kind of little white lie that crosses the line between charming and delusional and slightly bonkers.

I'm not interested

Unwanted attention is a horrible thing, whether it's that creepy dude in accounts who wears a lemon yellow cardigan and leaves you little love notes in your expenses forms, or a guy in a club who won't leave you alone until you slow dance with him. When this happens to you, your instinctive reaction will, of course, be to sneer "As if!" at him, but this is not, repeat NOT, fabulous behavior. Rudeness is not part of the sexy bitch's repertoire.

When getting rid of losers, be like a good mild shampoo: gentle yet effective. You don't want to be so polite you waste valuable man-hunting time on an unsuitable man, but equally you don't want to come across as a dragon because suitable men might see/hear of your bad behavior and be put off by it.

Body language is powerful without being confrontational. Withholding eye contact will scare most men off. Crossing your arms will make it even harder for them to approach you. Actually holding something between the two of you (newspaper, coat, large male friend) will create a barrier that even the most determined suitor will fear to cross. If he still doesn't get the message, a firm "I'm really not interested" will do.

And yet! If he takes it well, he might come in useful. You could fix him up with someone you know. He could be a valuable net-working partner. And, besides, it's always the ones you don't want to see who turn up everywhere you go, so parting on good terms means there's one less reason to skulk in dark corners.

when to move on and admit defeat

If he's already noticed you, he already likes the look of you, and all he needs is a little encouragement, then these techniques will have him eating out of your hand (or an altogether more interesting part of your anatomy, if you're lucky) before the night is through.

But they're not foolproof. Some nights, no matter how shiny our hair, how slinky our silhouette, the object of our desire won't desire us. It's a fact of life that not every man you like will like you. That's good news for me because otherwise you wouldn't be reading this book, but bad news for womankind in general, because rejection hurts, and a couple of setbacks in succession can dent your confidence to the point where you want to bow out of the dating game altogether.

The first rule is not to take a "no" personally, which seems like a gross contradiction in terms—after all, it's YOU he didn't want, so it must be YOU who is an unattractive failure destined to die alone, alone, alone, right? Not necessarily. He just didn't think you were right for him. Think of some of the men you've turned down in the past. Nice guys, not bad looking—they just didn't light your candle. Do you think there was anything inherently wrong about those men? No. You just realized that nice as he was, he wasn't the one for you, so you did him a favor by turning down his offer of a date and leaving him free to roam the world and find his soulmate. Now apply this thinking in reverse and you should feel a whole lot better next time it happens.

The next rule is an oldie but a goldie: If at first you don't succeed, try and try again. Think of the dating process in business terms. My friend Claire, a high-flying sales executive for a glossy magazine, says that for every 20 calls she makes, only one or two are successful. Claire's attitude to her job isn't clouded by emotion but clarified by the prospect of not earning her commission if she doesn't get any sales, but it makes perfect sense to apply her rule of "shoot more bullets, hit more targets" to dating. The more men you hit on, the easier it gets. By the time you chat up your tenth man of the week, you'll be so practiced at churning out those lines and fluttering those eyelashes, he'll be bowled over by your cool demeanor.

And the final, and golden, rule is to accept your rejection with good grace. Smile and say, "Ah, you can't win 'em all," and then drag the conversation out a little longer. After all, he could have a single friend just like him due to arrive any minute, who's been looking for a girl like you all his life....

we'll meet again

At the end of the evening, you'll know whether you want to see him again. Sometimes, it just happens—a slow dance turns into a kiss on the dance floor, he asks for your number with no prompting, you give it to him, you date, you live happily ever after. But the other 99 percent of the time, the course of true love doesn't run that smooth, and it's up to you to make sure you get together again.

Give him the opportunity to ask you out since most men would rather pursue than be pursued. If he doesn't, casually let him know that's what you'd like. Say, "It was really nice meeting you. We should keep in touch." Men are just as paranoid as we are and don't want to go out on a limb and ask you out if they think you might turn them down. If he still doesn't take the bait, take a deep breath and say, "Can I see you again?" Chances are he'll say yes.

But you're not home free yet. You've still got the obstacle of the telephone call to surmount. How do I get his number? Which number do I give out? When should I call him? And why do they say they'll call if they don't mean it? If these questions have ever occurred to you, congratulations, you're a woman.

Once it's been established you want to see each other again, it's perfectly acceptable to ask for his number, but again, waiting for him to ask for yours will make him feel macho and hunter-like. The easiest way to exchange numbers is to punch them into each other's cell phones at the end of the night, although if you do this I suggest a quick test call to make sure you've done it properly. Drunk fingers aren't renowned for their ability to hit the right key the first time, every time. If you want to give him more than one option, try slipping him your business card with your home phone number scrawled on the back in lipliner. This lets him know how fabulous and successful you are but the lipliner is a personal, feminine touch for him to remember you by. It goes without saying that if you only just met this guy in a club, it isn't a great idea to give him too much information— you don't want to make it *too* easy for him to turn stalker.

which number should you give out?

Do you slip him your work number, cell, home, fax, email, carrier pigeon? It goes without saying you shouldn't give them all out at once. Here's what the number you give out says about you.

work

Giving out your work number is a little cold and formal and might make him wonder what you've got to hide that you won't let him into your personal life. And besides, it might undermine your professionalism if you have to answer every work call with a breathy "Hello?" just in case it's him.

cell

These days most of us give out our cell numbers automatically and, of course, this is a great idea because it enables us to screen calls so we don't have to pick up if it's someone we don't want to talk to, or if "Will and Grace" is on. You can also ignore all his calls forever if you've changed your mind in the cold light of day. But be warned— a couple of my male friends say they don't like to call a girl on her cell in case she's busy or out with her mates, and simply resort to texting instead. While texting is a fast, fun, flirty and cheap way to get to know a potential stud, it's all too easy to get caught in the "text trap," a modern phenomenon whereby you both become used to hiding behind the safety of the text message and you never actually work up the courage to call each other and arrange to meet. Cell phones are also problematic in that, until the day they come with a built-in breathalyser, we tend to have them on our persons in bars, clubs and other places where the wine is flowing freely and your love interest is shuddently the mosht important pershon in the world and you shimply musht call him and tell him you love him THISH INSHTANT. There is currently no safeguarding against this. I think there's a gap in the market, don't you?

home

Giving out your home number will at least reassure him you're not already in a live-in relationship. Beware, though, if you have roommates and messages mysteriously disappear. It would be terrible shame to stall a beautiful friendship before it had a chance to begin. He'll only call a couple of times before getting disheartened. Cheesy comedy answering machine greetings are also a no-no, unless you want to go out with the kind of guy who wears ties with Disney characters on them. That said, the other extreme—the automated voice messaging service your phone company provides you with—is too impersonal. Have a straight-forward recorded message that explains you're not around but you'll

On your home phone, you will be able to have lots of fun with Caller ID, which lets you know everyone who's called you and their phone numbers, even those who didn't leave a message. If you're calling from home, *67 (or 1167 on a rotary phone) lets you withhold your identity from the person you're calling in case they have Caller ID, too. But then there's *69, the magic number that automatically dials the last number you received. So you might want to think twice about doing the dial-and-hang-up. Withholding your number is very useful if you don't want him to know your home number just yet (maybe you want to wait until after the date before you can stop screening him through your cell phone). It's rare for men to withhold their number, but if he does, warning bells should ring. Either he's a manipulator who wants to pull all the strings or he's totally neurotic and can't bear the idea of you knowing as much about him as he does about you. And call me old-fashioned, but I think it's the woman's prerogative to be the neurotic one in the relationship.

call back as soon as you are. And, if you have a male roomie, try not to let him record it. If you were calling him, how would you feel encountering a sultry female voice on his answering machine?

fax

Faxing can be quite fun in a retro-'80s-yuppie way. Sending a message by fax combines the personal touch of your own handwriting with the instant impact of "modern" technology. However, unless he works alone or in a very small, informal office, make sure the information isn't something you mind at least 20 of his co-workers seeing as it rolls out of the machine. He might be a huge fan of your breasts, but faxing a picture of them to his strait-laced law firm isn't going to do his professionalism or his feelings for you any good whatsoever. And if he gets caught clogging up the work fax with personal correspondence, he might get the sack, and how's he going to be able to take you to dinner at upscale restaurants then?

email

Email is a blessing and a curse. There's something wildly thrilling about cyber-banter with a new man. For a start, the luxury of time lets you say things that are far wilder and wittier than you'd ever muster in a conversation. It stops clockwatching in the office and makes the time fly by, although it might be hard to explain your sudden lack of productivity to your boss, and you must be aware that your company can access your emails whenever it sees fit. And another caveat: like text flirting, email flirting can be addictive as you start to wonder whether you'll be able to live up to the funny sex-bomb persona you've created online.

when to call and who should

I'm not going to bullshit you—this is the hard part. This is that point where the dating game becomes a waiting game and is perhaps the most stressful part of the process. In theory, who calls who first depends on who pursued whom. If he asked for your number, he should call you. If you took his, the ball's in your court.

At some point, even the most fabulous sexy bitch has been driven to distraction by a seemingly perfect man who promised he'd call and then didn't. Honey, if there were a real solution to this problem, then someone else would have discovered and published it years ago and would perhaps have been able to buy a small country with the proceeds. The only answer I can come up with is that sometimes it's easier for a man to say "I'll call you" than to say "Look, I'm taking your number because I think it might be a little awkward not to, and when I'm sober I'll realize I don't really want to see you after all." "I'll call you" then, can be used as a line to end a socially awkward situation. It's often easy to predict whether he'll ring your bell or not by analyzing what he says. A dismissive, vague "I'll call you" doesn't tell you much. But in my experience, guys who are specific and say something like "I'll call you next week—is Tuesday evening a good time to talk to you?" mean business.

A couple of days after your first meeting is the ideal first point of contact. You'll still be fresh in each other's memories at this point, but you'll have had a couple of days to do the important stuff like discuss the situation in great detail with all of your friends and imagine each other naked.

If he leaves it any more than a week, that's a wee bit insensitive, not to mention foolish—doesn't this guy realize that wild things run fast and that if he doesn't move quickly, he could lose you? Probably not. It's more likely that he didn't want to seem too eager, or that it took him so long to pluck up the courage to dial your number that after a while, he felt the deadline had passed and wimped out of calling you altogether. This happens more often than you'd think. One of the guys I was in college with once got so worked up about calling a girl he'd met that he was physically sick every time he tried to call her.

Give him the benefit of the doubt and, if seven days pass without a word, give him a call. Freak the dude out by remaining bright, breezy and just a little bit flirty, but don't ask him why he hasn't been in contact with you yet—you want to let him know it's still OK for him to keep in touch with you without bullying him into seeing you.

And after that, don't wait by the phone for a single minute more. *So* easier said than done. We've all done it—waited by both phones for him to ring, only to call ourselves on the cell phone to check both it and the landline are working, and then when they are, we convince ourselves that he must have called in that three seconds when both lines of communication were busy.

But if he likes you, he'll call back. It's that simple. Don't worry about being hard to pin down: He's far more likely to want to chase a fabulous girl-about-town than a girl who doesn't leave the house for days on end. If you're always in, he'll think, "Why doesn't she have anything better to do than wait by the phone? What's wrong with her? If we get together, is she going to want me to sit in front of the TV with her every night for the rest of my life?" Be a little bit elusive, on the other hand, and he'll be thinking, "Who's she out with? I bet she's fighting off the guys with a stick tonight. I'd better get her while she's still single." His imagination does all the hard work so you don't have to.

the call

With all the stress and worry of who calls, where and when, it's easy to lose sight of the most important part—the actual making of the telephone call and arranging of the date. And before you speak to him, there's something you should know. Men tend to see the telephone as a tool of communication that has no purpose beyond the functional. They really don't see the point in talking for any length of time when you can have a conversation, say, in a bar. For him, the fact that you spoke at all means more than how long the conversation lasted. How fucked up is that? So during your conversation, err on the side of brevity and keep the conversation short and sweet, leaving him wanting more of you. Save the awkward pauses for your face-to-face meeting when you can cover them up with body language!

When you're trying to get him to agree to a date, don't *umm* and *aah* and say, "I don't know—you choose." Be receptive to his suggestions, but if he doesn't have any, have your own specific ideas up your street. Don't be vague. Suggest dinner on Tuesday or a drink after work on Wednesday and let him choose the venue. That way, it's still a mutual decision AND he can only say "yes" or "no" to the dates you've suggested. If he's unavailable but eager, he'll suggest another date. If he's unavailable and vague about when he can see you, don't hold your breath and get out with your dignity intact, leaving it up to him to call you again if he wants to see you.

4 do your homework

So you've landed your date. Well done. I'm proud of you.

But before you embark on your adventure, you need a little careful forward planning to remove those little obstacles to a perfect first date, like late arrivals, inappropriate clothes and awkward silences. The better-prepared you know you are, the more relaxed you'll be on the date itself. And the more relaxed you are on the date itself, the lower your chances are of being a nervous wreck who drinks too much, too quickly and spills her soup in her lap.

Choosing how to spend your date should in theory be up to the person who did the asking. Traditionally it's always been the man's job, but we've already established that dating in the 21st century has nothing to do with tradition. That said, I'm invariably happy to abdicate this responsibility and let the man decide where we're going and what we're doing. This is because I'm essentially lazy, and because I think that he's likely to suggest somewhere new I've never been before. In fact, it's my pet peeve when a man asks me out, calls me up and then doesn't have any idea about what he wants to do with me (apart from the obvious, that is). Freakin' useless. Whenever I challenge men about this, they say they didn't want to seem too old-fashioned and bossy by dictating where we went, so it's wise to have a couple of venues in mind in case he doesn't.

Location, location, location. The first thing you need to establish is where you're going on your date because this affects everything else about it. Important factors like what you're going to wear, how you're going to behave, how much it's going to cost you depend on your venue.

The adventure you embark on depends on a lot of things, like what you already know you've got in common, where you both live, how much time you've got and how sure you are you like this guy.

early-evening drinks in a bar

Easily the most popular location for city dating, and it's easy to see why. At least 50 percent of the time we have no idea whether our drinking partner is a potential boyfriend or potential plutonic friend, and this kind of date could go either way. If it's clear halfway through the evening, that despite the social lubricant that is five mojitos, he's not the man for you, you can make your excuses and slip out in a way that more formal dates just don't allow without you compromising your legendary sexy bitch poise and cool. If, on the other hand, you're rubbing along nicely, then you can move on to dinner, a movie or a club to get to know each other better. Your early-evening drink can turn out to be the perfect launchpad for what lies ahead. It's true that "meeting up for a beer to see how things go" is about as informal as a date can be. Now, there is a school of thought that says the more you like someone, the more formal the date will be, and that the more effort we go through in terms of choosing a venue and grooming ourselves, the more serious we are about our new special friend. This is true to a certain extent, and I reckon if he takes you for a drink in a posh new wine bar he can't afford, he's out to impress. But I don't think you should take his suggestion to meet you in the pub opposite his office after work as a sign that he doesn't care. After all, this says he's confident enough in the rapport you've already built to see him in his work clothes, *and* he isn't worried about the prospect of his workmates seeing him out with you.

concert

There's nothing as reassuring as discovering your chosen guy has the same taste in music as you, which is why concerts are very make-or-break. Music tastes are a huge indicator of how compatible your lifestyles are going to be. Sometimes a Faith Hill fan and a Marilyn Manson fan will find true and everlasting love, but more often than not, it's a sign of disharmony to come. Concerts are great for posing as you can really dress up in the name of rock 'n' roll—whether you're a hip-hop honey or a college rock chick, you get to go right out there and express your inner sexy bitch. The smaller and more intimate the venue the better since everyone looks sexy through the smoky haze of underground jazz clubs, but not even the loveliest lady looks her best underneath the fluorescent lighting of a big-city stadium. Everyone's packed in so tightly that you'll be snuggling up against each other out of necessity, which is delicious, and if you're lucky, he'll come and rescue you from the moshpit when things get sweaty. If, however, you're after deep and interesting conversation, you're out of luck because the decibel level means you have to shout in each others ears to make yourself heard. Inevitably, five minutes into the conversation you lose the ability to understand a word he's saying, and throw your head back and laugh at his every unintelligible comment. Which is kind of embarrassing when he's just asked, "Do you know where the bathroom is?"

movie theater

Seeing a movie together immediately gives you something in common and can spark off conversation like nothing else. But how do you decide which film to see? Something too girlie and he'll be bored. Something too guysville and you'll be asleep before the action hero even strips down to his grubby white undershirt. A lot of us assume that an arthouse movie will make us look sophisticated and worldly, but that has its pitfalls, too. I once took a new man to see the Italian classic *Cinema Paradiso,* only to find out later that he was dyslexic and hadn't been able to follow the subtitles. Unless you have a very clear idea of his tastes, go for whatever's on the front cover of this month's film magazines. Timing is also important when you're going to the movies since it's important that when the closing credits roll, you can go somewhere for coffee, a bite to eat, or an alcoholic drink. There's something a little disconcerting about leaving the movie theater at the best of times and being thrust back into real life—you at least want to go somewhere and wind down/talk about things/re-enact the heart-stopping screen kiss from the final frame, and it's not very easy to do that when everything's shutting down and you have to catch the last subway or go pick up your car from the lot before your permit expires.

theater

Like the movies, it'll give you something to talk about, but theater is more of an occasion date. That said, these days a trip to the theater could be anything from some avant-garde experimental comedy in an auditorium the size of a closet to a Broadway extravaganza. If your date invited you to an upscale production, he's either so incredibly posh and rich he takes this kind of thing for granted, or he's really out to impress. Judge for yourself by listening to how he talks and seeing how expensive his shoes are. A night at the opera can be incredibly romantic—think back to that scene in *Pretty Woman* where Richard Gere takes Julia Roberts to see *La Traviata* and she absolutely melted? If you're worried you won't be able to hold your own with the high-brow post-theater conversation, cheat by reading all the reviews you can get your hands on and steal your opinion from one of the critics.

comedy clubs

The ultimate cheap and cheerful night. Just don't, for god's sake, do what I did on an early date with my boyfriend and sit in front because you *will* be picked on and there's nothing a comedian likes more than a first-date couple. Opt for the latest possible performance; if it's funny, it'll put you both in a great mood—the endorphins you release when you laugh send the same hormone as the ones you get when you're falling in love coursing around your body, so it'll compound all your romantic feelings for each other. Humor is very important in a relationship so this is a chance to go and check out what makes him laugh. Warning bells should ring if your date sits stony-faced through the gags that have you wetting your panties with mirth, or laughs at the sexiest asshole who seems to be going for the world record in offending the largest number of people in the shortest span of time.

restaurant rendezvous

This is the second most common choice of date for urban singletons. It's the most traditional way of getting to know each other. In fact, dinner-a-deux in a restaurant is one of the only occasions when we know exactly where we stand. It's a formal, structured environment, and encourages us to be on our best behavior.

It goes without saying that certain foods should be avoided on a first date. I, for one, have never finished a plate of spaghetti bolognese without at least half of it ending up splattered on my chest and face, and have smiled sweetly across a dinner table to reveal spinach-festooned teeth more often than I care to remember. Garlic is an all-or-nothing food. Either both of you eat it or neither of you touch it because of its unparalleled ability to make your breath smell. Onions and chili will have the same effect, but with chili you get the added bonus of having a hot flush, too, and watching your make-up slide right off your face—from Sexy Bitch to Sweaty Bitch in the time it takes to bite right into a jalapeno pepper. A light green salad can freshen your breath, but don't go overboard on the fruit and veggies—high-fiber stuff like broccoli and cauliflower will bloat your tummy and make you fart.

A lot of women make the mistake of refusing to eat on a date, thinking that he'll find it so much sexier to see them picking at their Caesar salad than wolfing down a T-bone steak. Not so—men love women who aren't afraid of food (my theory is that once they see you like to put things in your mouth, their sexual imagination will start working overtime). If you're so nervous you can't eat much, opt for a cuisine where you order a variety of dishes and share them, like Spanish tapas, Chinese dim sum or Turkish meze. Because you're not just clearing a plate, it's hard for him to gauge how much you're eating. Happily, this also means you can gorge loads and get away with it, too.

Sharing food also lets you share the experience—and you can feed each other, which is a playful way to initiate physical contact. It's worth learning how to use chopsticks even if it's just so you can sexily pop a wonton in his mouth. A few years ago, I went on a work dinner to an incredibly swank Chinese restaurant and was mortified when I was the only one who had to resort to a knife and fork. For weeks afterward, I practiced eating my morning cornflakes with chopsticks. Now, I'm so dexterous with a pair of them, I can virtually crochet a packet of noodles into a nice scarf.

cooking for you at home

Personally, I'd be a little wary of any guy who suggests you go over to his place for take-out Chinese and a DVD for your first date. It could, of course, be that he's hypnotized by your body and DES-PERATE to get you into bed. Hey, he's only male. If this is the case, he's banking on the fact that you'll think it's easier to make the transition from vertical to horizontal if the bedroom door is only a couple of feet away from the sofa you've been making out on. Flattering but awkward if you don't feel the same way. But then there's also the strong possibility that he's simply too cheap to pay for a date, and if he isn't willing to make that small effort at this early stage of the dating game where men are always on their best, out-to-impress-her behavior, warning bells should be ringing loud and clear in your head. I don't care if he makes Tobey Maguire look like a jackass—if you get along well, you have forever to eat home-cooked risotto in front of the TV. Sexy bitches should be on the lookout for a guy who pulls out all the stops in the first few months of the relationship. The whole point of going out with someone is, well, to go out with him.

Also, on a personal safety note, is it really such a great idea to go to a guy's apartment when you don't really know the first thing about him? Nu-uh.

theme parks

There's nothing like goofing off work and getting a ticket to your local thrills-and-spills theme park, for making you act and feel like a pair of besotted teenagers. The scary rides boost your heart rate and get the adrenaline pounding, mimicking the effects of the first flush of love and adding to that dizzy first-date feeling. He can satisfy his masculine hunter-gatherer instincts by winning you a huge stuffed bear at a stall, and you can make out and grope like a pair of hormonal teens in the ghost train. The only real drawback is that this first date doesn't really mix with alcohol, so if you're the kind of chick who needs a little "courage" when you're out with a new man, it's best avoided. Don't be tempted. It might seem quite romantic sneaking a bottle of champagne and plastic glasses into the tunnel of love, but when you're hurtling upside down at 200 mph on a rollercoaster, it will suddenly be the worst idea you ever had. There's only one bodily fluid he's interested in—and it ain't vomit.

historical sites

Plunging into a different time period—even for 20 minutes—can be an incredibly liberating experience; getting away from the rat race and losing yourself in history. Every large city has some random tourist attraction you've driven past a million times but never bothered to go see—whether it's the birthplace of a Great American, a beautiful old building that looks like its straight out of a movie set or a museum devoted to obscure indigenous people. Those awful places you used to be dragged to on school trips are so much more fun when you swap your teachers and your worksheets for an eligible bachelor and have a day to wander around your local stately home, imagining yourselves rich aristocrats. Take even the most urbane young man out of the city and put him into a little slice of history and let him discover his chivalrous streak—he'll be putting his coat in puddles so you don't have to spoil your shoes and, with a bit of luck, this treat-her-like-a-lady attitude will extend to a souvenir ruler from the gift shop and lunch in the quaint themed cafe. I'm warning you now that you'll do well to invest in a pair of flat shoes, though, or the date will start with you spiking a hole through the 200-year-old wooden floor of a handbuilt pioneer cabin.

not on a school night

The night you choose for your date says as much about your expectations as the venue…

saturday

It's an encouraging sign if a man is willing to give up Saturday night for you but be warned it's likely to be quite formal: this is excellent if you're an old-fashioned girl who wants to be wined and dined, less so if you'd rather keep things casual until you're sure you like him. Of course, the main advantage that a Saturday-night date offers is that it gives you the whole day in which to pamper, preen and prepare yourself so that you can present him with a body of utter bootyliciousness. That and the fact that if all goes well you can spend a lazy, lusty Sunday in bed together.

midweek

Say you meet your guy on a Saturday night and agree to meet one night after work in the coming week. So far, so good. "School nights" have much to recommend them.

You can go somewhere casual, just for a drink, and see what develops from there. Far better to get intimate in a little red velvet–lined booth over a bottle of wine than in a big, bright, noisy, modern restaurant. Or you can go to a bar and get something to eat later if that grabs you. If halfway through the night you don't like him, you can cut the evening short and pretend you were just a couple of friends out for drinks and let him know that (see "At the End of the Date" in Chapter 5).

The awful thing about drinks after work is that you take the day's stresses, strains and underarm sweat patches along to the date with you, but these usually evaporate after a couple of glasses of Rioja and a little bit of handholding. So which night do you go out? Mondays, for a start, are off limits. Mondays are hard enough without the stress of a first date at the end of it all. And if you met him on the weekend, where the hell is your hard-to-get instinct? Tuesday is also a little too soon—you don't want him to think you have nothing better to do than jump and say yes as soon as he calls. So as far as he's concerned, you're busy on Tuesdays, too. Wednesday or Thursday are much better, giving the pair of you a few dates to think about and anticipate, but not so long the momentum drops off or you get carried away with building up a picture he'll never live up to.

friday

At first glance, Friday nights don't seem ideal for first dates. Wiped out after a long working week, surely you'd rather be out with your co-workers, bitching about your boss, or at home, slumped in front of the tube with a pizza and hoping something good will be on. But hey—Friday combines the anything-could-happen vibe of a weekday with the possibility of spending the whole weekend screwing each other's brains out. What does it say about his intentions if he asks you out on a Friday night? Judge it by how much effort it's going to take and how much time you'll be able to spend alone. If he's just asked you to tag along with his work buddies, it could be that he sees you as one of the guys and can't even be bothered to set aside a night to get to know you. If he's openly affectionate with you in front of his colleagues, however, that's obviously not the case.

sunday

Coffee or afternoon drinks at a bar seems to be an increasingly common first-date choice, and there's no doubt that this lazy, leisurely way of getting to know each other can be utterly delicious. You'll have lots to talk about—what you've done with your weekend so far, your working week and the contents of the Sunday papers. In short, it's the perfect way to spend a day with a man you've been seeing for a couple of months. But as first dates go, Sundays don't really encourage much passion. Sure, by putting ourselves in this potentially platonic situation we're not really running the risk of rejection but we're also reducing our chances of making a move. A few years ago I spent a lovely Sunday drinking red wine, eating a big roast dinner and chatting over the Sunday papers with a man I'd met at a wedding a couple of months earlier. We got along famously, but there wasn't much scope for tactile flirting across a big table and the Style section. No problem, I reasoned—I invited him home for coffee in the hope things would progress there. I arrived home only to find my roommate and her boyfriend watching the TV with an empty pizza box and empty beer bottles and stubbed-out cigarettes everywhere. Needless to say, the moment was gone. If that's not enough to put you off, remember that Sundays are the morning after the night before. One or both of you could arrive hungover and irritable or, worst case scenario, have met someone else the night before.

Case the joint

Check out where you're going a couple of days before the date itself. No self-respecting burglar would try to commit a bank heist at a bank he wasn't familiar with, and the same level of research is required of you. Not only should you be familiar with the best way to get there and back (for personal safety as well as timekeeping reasons), but you'll feel more relaxed if you've had a peek at the menu and the clientele beforehand. Don't underestimate the importance of getting the dress code right since not being allowed in a club because you're wearing jeans, or feeling overdressed in a hip, shabby-chic bar, will wreck your evening.

This is especially true if he's suggested where to meet. I know that an urban sophisticate like you is well aware of basic restaurant etiquette, but if you've landed a man who's out to impress, you could find yourself confronted with the newest, trendiest place in town. That could be a private club that looks like someone's front door, or that new Korean/Finnish fusion restaurant that got a rave review in some style bible last week.

Casing the joint will also enable you to plan your journey. This is important for a couple of reasons. Working out your route means you can make sure you get there on time (or ten minutes late, if you want to keep him sweating).

Doing a "test run" of your journey to the date is also vital for your personal safety. If you're driving, you want to find the nearest, well-lit parking lot that's near enough the venue so you can walk there in your Jimmy Choos, and is well-lit and staffed in case you get back real late. Big-city parking lots tend to be underground and are not the kinds of places a sexy bitch likes to wander around in at 2 a.m. on her own. If you're drinking, then it's even more important to look after yourself. While I'd always recommend getting a cab home, sometimes it's not always financially viable or practical do this on the way to the date because it costs so damn much or because in rush hour it's so much quicker to walk or take the bus. Rehearsing your journey means you can anticipate potential mine-fields like subway connections that involve a three-mile underground hike in your high heels, or bus stops in dark, scary places that are best avoided.

take care of yourself

Basic safety precautions are a must on any date with a man you don't know too well yet. Some of them might seem a little over the top, but when it comes to looking after yourself, it's always best to err on the side of caution.

Always let someone—your roommate or pick-up partner—know exactly where you're going and what time to expect you back. Get her to give you a call at an appointed time to check you're OK. Keep your cell phone switched on at all times and don't be afraid to let him know it's there. Make a point of switching it to silent or vibrate so he knows you don't want your classy Yankee Doodle ringtone disturbing your lovely evening, but he also knows you're reachable. Don't be embarrassed: A decent guy will understand that you're only looking after yourself, and will admire and respect you because of it. Put his mind at ease by explaining what you're doing and that you always do it. That way, he'll know it's just part of your first-date ritual and nothing personal, that you're not just doing it because his eyebrows meet in the middle.

Always meet somewhere public and well-lit. Don't let him pick you up at home if you don't know him very well, and certainly avoid going to his place on a first date. If you wouldn't be comfortable letting him pick you up at home, don't let him meet you at the office, either. It's worth noting that a nice guy will always care about how you get home, even if he hasn't had so much as a peck on the cheek. If he's happy to leave you half-drunk at the cab stand or subway station, he's a prick and doesn't deserve a second date.

It's better to be ten minutes late than ten minutes early. As well as keeping him on his toes and getting him whipped up into a frenzy of joyful anticipation, it's better for a man to hang around on his own in a strange place than for a woman.

Much has been made of drug rape—the sinister practice of guys spiking girls' drinks with untraceable sedatives that'll cause her to not know what's going on. Though you can get a variety of things from coasters to swizzle sticks that'll test for the presence of these drugs in your drink, the easiest way to defend yourself against this is to buy your drinks yourself and to watch them and never leave them alone.

Carry a personal alarm. This tiny device is smaller than a trial-size can of hairspray and will make a screeching wee waa noise that'll deter anyone you use it on. They're cheap and easily obtainable from drugstores.

purse rules

While make-up is your warpaint, your purse is your weapon and should contain all you need to keep yourself a) beautiful and b) safe during and after your date. I'm a huge purse fan, largely because I own at least 50 and none of them have ever made my butt look bigger. Use your purse to make a statement and express your personality in a way you wouldn't always be able to through your clothes: for example, sometimes I'm in a hippy chick kind of mood, but I don't want to wear henna tattoos, a peasant blouse and pigtails, so I'll accessorize an otherwise plain outfit with a patchwork mirrorwork bag I bought in India, and I've made my point. The same outfit with, say, a Louis Vuitton clutch bag would make me look much richer and more sophisticated than I really am.

Your purse mantra is "Downsize, downsize and then downsize some more." Large purses are bad date material for many reasons, not least the havoc carrying a heavy shoulderbag will wreak on your posture. Turning up to your date with a huge holdall slung over your shoulder will have him worrying what the hell you've got in it. A video camera? A beginner's bondage kit? A relationship contract in 300 easy-to-read pages? A flannel nightgown? Your teddy bear? Men, most of whom can fit everything they need for the night in their pants pockets, are mystified by the need for handbags in the first place—and in a women-are-crazy way rather than a feminine, alluring one.

My oldest girlfriend Claire is currently living out of town with her parents while she saves up for an apartment of her own. This could seriously impede her sexy bitch lifestyle if she weren't so damned organized. She spends roughly three nights a week crashing on someone's couch and has the purse thing down to a fine art. We were in a cocktail bar a few weeks ago when her cell phone rang. She delved into a handbag that looked on the outside about the size of a VHS tape and out flew a small tube of Tums; a planner; an electric toothbrush still in its original carrying case; cleanser, toner and moisturizer; tampons; spare pantyhose and a travel hairdryer. But those of us who don't have a Mary Poppins–like ability to pull the contents of our apartments out of our purses should only carry the following essentials.

Condoms: You already know all the reasons why. If you don't, I'm afraid I'm gonna have to send you back to sexy bitch school since you clearly didn't graduate last time.

Make-up: A little powder to blot out shine and something to re-touch your lips is all you need in your make-up bag, and if your look requires a higher level of maintenance than that, go to the bathroom, wipe it all off and start again until your look is suitably low-mainte-nance (see below for why he'll love you for it).

Cell phone and a refill card if your phone is pay-as-you-go. A list of cab numbers in your city that you know you can rely on. It's good to have a company with a large network of cabs that covers the whole of your city in case you end up in an unfamiliar area or—heaven forbid—the suburbs.

A toothbrush and mini toothpaste for freshening up between courses or, more importantly, the morning after. If you have smelly morning breath, neither of you are going to want a repeat performance.

Cash and cards, at least enough for the maximum possible cab fare, and enough to pay for half of all drinks, food, tips, etc.

Baby wipes. A travel-sized pack of these is a dating girl's most versatile product. They can cleanse and moisturize in one swoop and even fix eye make-up, and double up as deodorizing wipes for your underarms and between your legs if you don't have access to a shower.

dressing for your date

The clothes you wear for your date are very different from the ones you wore to seduce him in the first place. You should be aiming for a slightly toned-down version of the way you looked when he first noticed you. Why? Well, it's not a great idea to dress as though you're giving him sex on a plate by showing acres of flesh and wearing make-up that wouldn't look out of place on a porn star. Even if you are offering him sex on a plate, he wants to think he's earned it, and it's a shame to shatter the illusion. He'll spend a fair amount of time imagining what you look like naked as part of the anticipation of the sex to follow. Let him indulge that fantasy. Besides, not many man are comfortable with their dates parading around as if in prowl mode for other men to see. It'll be buried deep in his subconscious, but he's already feeling a little possessive of you.

If you do want to wear something that expresses how wanton, sluttish and downright sexy this new guy makes you feel, then do it beneath your clothes. Go all-out for glamour on the underwear front. And by that I don't just mean wear matching bra and panties. Clad yourself in beautiful, expensive lingerie rather than the black-and-red nylon peephole variety—if he likes that, he'll let you know soon enough, trust me.

Instead, aim for understated elegance and let him know you've made an effort—clean hair and ironed clothes are vital. If you've come straight from the office, let him know you've freshened up before by re-applying your make-up and maybe changing your clothes.

If it's a weekend date, make sure you're wearing something that's as flattering as it is comfortable. It's tempting to make a bold statement with your outfit, but just at the beginning, let your personality rather than your clothes make the big impression.

If you don't know what flatters you, pretend you have a big wedding/job interview coming up and have a personal shopper take you around your city's classiest department store. Most of the big stores offer this service for free, or at least offset against the cost of your purchase. Whether you buy something or not, you'll get some great advice on what works for you in terms of colors and styles.

Wearing something new can boost your confidence but it's a mistake to go shopping for clothes on the day of your date as you'll inevitably panic-buy something that doesn't suit or fit you. You'll spend the whole evening feeling uncomfortable and he'll wonder why you're tugging furiously at the offending garment, trying to make it go away. Stick with a look you know works for you and jazz it up with a new bag or pair of shoes. And as an extra insurance, get a friend whose dress sense you approve of and whose judgment you trust to OK your date outfit before you go.

There are practical issues to consider, too. For example, don't wear white unless you plan to be eating and drinking transparent things all night. All it takes is one red wine splash on your left nipple to make you feel self-conscious all evening.

If you plan to get naked later on that night, you need easy-access clothes that can be slipped on and off with the minimum of fuss (see page 104 in Chapter 6 for my tips on stripping). And while style is paramount, comfort is important, too. I'm not suggesting you pop out and invest in a pair of jeans with an elastic waist (as that would be contrary to all you stand for as a sexy bitch), but if you are wearing pants, make sure you can actually move/sit down. It's all very well wearing a pair of butt-hugging leather trousers that look great when you're standing up, but after a meal or a few glasses of wine your belly will bloat and when you remove those pants, you'll have a rather unlovely red imprint of the waistband on your skin. Shop around and find a pair of Magic Black Pants made from stretch fabric that make your legs look fabulous. Gap and Banana Republic have the best range of Magic Black Pants.

Make-up should be minimal, and you want to look healthy rather than vampish. Use foundation and concealer to cover blemishes rather than to change the color of your skin. Use blusher to give you a healthy glow, but don't be fooled into thinking you can sculpt cheekbones with it. Keep lips defined but natural-looking, and whatever you're doing, don't turn up with a high-maintenance, glossy pout he's too scared to kiss. Tidy up your eyebrows and slick on a coat of mascara that's just a couple of shades darker than your natural lash color.

Nails should be short, neat and natural-looking. You can bet your Fendi handbag that every time he looks at your hands he's wondering where you're going to put them later on, so don't scare him off with inch-long red talons. He might like the idea of having his back scratched, but not his jewels.

While we're on the subject of grooming, it's important to insert a line about your body hair. Fuzz-free legs and armpits are a must if there's even the slightest chance your man is going to be running his hands over your bare skin. Ignore this advice at your peril—it's only natural that the days when you venture out with stubbly armpits, gorilla legs and saggy gray grandma underwear are inevitably the days Brad Pitt's sexier, younger brother wants to take you to bed for a three-hour love marathon….

As for the bikini line, the last time I flipped through a men's magazine, the girls posing in bikinis didn't seem to possess a pubic hair between them, but don't let yourself be bullied into putting yourself through the agony of a Brazilian wax—I interviewed a nude model a while back and she says none of the girls would dream of using anything other than a depilatory cream. Yeah, you could be so fascistic about body hair that you have your bikini line waxed on a fortnightly basis, but that would fill your life with endless booking appointments and exfoliating to avoid icky ingrown hairs. Despite what beauty magazines tell you, guys don't expect you to drop your drawers to reveal a little Hitler moustache and acres of smooth skin.

In fact, they'd probably be a little alarmed if you did. A little pubic hair never hurt anyone.

But notice I said "a little pubic hair"—while you don't have to be a slave to hot wax, he doesn't want to be confronted with a bush so big the government wants to turn it into a national park. A little trimming won't go amiss—what's the point of spending $30 bucks on a pair of hipster panties if, when you put them on, you look like you're smuggling a Yorkshire terrier in them? You don't need to go for the boiled-egg look, but keeping your pubic area neat and tidy by trimming with nail scissors or even an electric nose-hair trimmer means you'll look more groomed. I also think the less hair down there, the more sensitive you'll be to his every touch—and let's face it, girls, anything that makes it easier for him to see what he's doing can only be a good thing.

gross beauty tricks

Isn't it great when you have a date on a Saturday night and you start getting ready at lunchtime—lavender bath with a glass of wine, face pack, hair treatment, and a couple of hours to buff your body to baby-smoothness? Yes, it is. And it's horrific when you've agreed to meet your date at eight o'clock on a Wednesday night but your meeting finished at 6:30 and by the time you get home, you barely have time to take a shower, let alone run a bath. Luckily, there are some rather unorthodox quick-fixes to tide you over…

Talcum powder lightly shaken over the roots of your hair and then brushed through absorbs grease when you don't have time to wash your hair.

Need a pedicure but can't be bothered with buffing and slough-ing? When you're in the bath or shower, take a disposable razor and scrape off the worst of the dead skin, then massage Vaseline into your feet.

Vaseline can also serve as a last-minute split-end repair job.

Bags under the eyes can be eradicated with a slick of hemorrhoid cream. Yes, really. The magic ingredient that soothes the skin of your—ahem—anus also has a calming effect on the equally delicate skin under your eyes.

A run in your sheer pantyhose? Clear nail polish will stop it from running more until you can slip into a new pair.

Hole in your thick winter opaque pantyhose? I've been known to use a marker to color my legs in to match my tights. It works great, but needless to say, it's not the best method if you plan to disrobe in front of your man that evening.

Bare-legged? A wet tea bag brushed lightly over your legs acts as a subtle fake tan. Be very gentle when you're applying it, though, unless you want to end up with tea leaves all over your legs—that's NOT the look you're going for.

A spray-on fabric freshener like Febreze can deodorize hair that's rank with last night's bar smoke, but this one *really* is for emergencies only—these products aren't known for their conditioning properties!

5 tonight's the night

a little more conversation, a little less action

So you're all dolled up with somewhere to go, waiting for the cab to whisk you off to your venue—and you're paralyzed with pre-date jitters. It's only natural that you get excited—in fact, if you were utterly blasé, there wouldn't be much point in the date in the first place. But even the sexiest of bitches needs to be able to relax into the evening and be yourself or you'll give off an air of psychotic desperation that will have him scratching his head and wondering what happened to that funny, laidback girl he spoke to on the phone.

Before you even approach your date, do some breathing exercises to warm up your voice. Your mouth might be a little dry, especially if you're nervous and haven't spoken to anyone for a while. Both these things can cause your voice to tremble, meaning your opening gambit comes out all strangled. Sing scales or a verse of your favorite song, say "a e i o u" over and over until your vocal cords are warm and there's no chance of this. It's better to do this in the ladies room or the taxi than while you're waiting alone at your table or in the foyer of the movie theater, by the way.

Hide your nerves by method acting. It sounds crazy, but if you tell yourself you're confident often enough and pretend that you're oozing with sass and self-esteem, you'll project an air of confidence and before long, it'll be true. If you really are nervous, whatever you do, don't resort to that oft-recommended trick of imagining the person who's making you nervous without his clothes on. When you're already dizzy with nerves and sick with lust, do you really think it's going to be anything other than wildly distracting to imagine your companion topless? And imagine the blush on your cheeks when you start thinking about the parts of his body hidden below the tablecloth…it certainly won't have the calming, soothing effect you're after.

One of the reasons we're so nervous is because we're worried he won't like us, which is a healthy sign because it's a waste of time to date men you don't want to impress. But remember that a date is a two-way process. Sure, you want to make a good impression on him, but remember, he also needs to meet your approval. You'll find that if you keep thinking "I hope I like you" rather than "I hope you like me," you'll relax into the experience much more.

You found out the basics when you were hitting on each other. Now's the time to delve a little deeper, get to know each other more intimately and gauge whether you're as compatible as you seemed on that dance floor, and whether you'd like to take things further. And there's only one way to do this: talking. And lots of it.

A lot of us quite rightly hate small talk. It can be awkward, a little artificial and dull. But it's necessary. Think of small talk as the foreplay before the sex of the deep and meaningful conversations.

Launching straight into your extreme views on the Israel-Palestine conflict or capital punishment and you'll make a strong impression for all the wrong reasons. Small talk is a necessary warm-up exercise to figure out each other's sensibilities. You can also use this time where nothing of particular consequence is being said to observe him and see what turns you on—or off—about him.

If you're really going to be stuck for something to say, fill up your small-talk reservoir before you go out. Read a couple of newspapers while you're waiting for your toenail polish to dry. Have a variety on hand, from downmarket supermarket trash like the *National Enquirer* to *Time* magazine. Guys, I'm afraid to say, still tend to wildly underestimate sexy bitches: Some of the most enlightened men I've met have been shocked that women would ever be interested in, let alone able to hold a conversation about, anything other than celebrities and make-up. So read up on everything from the Space Race to Stephen Hawking's last book to this week's big movie releases.

Or if that sounds too much like hard work, steer the conversation around to his favorite subject—himself. He probably doesn't get the chance to relax and do that with his friends, as male conversation tends to be based around humor and point scoring, so providing a sympathetic ear will hugely endear you to him.

How best to tease this information out of him? Well, there's a fine line between asking some leading questions that'll have him opening up to you and grilling him as though you were interviewing him for a job or a dating agency. The trick is to ask him questions about general aspects of his private life but stop him before it gets too personal. For example, asking him where he went on his last couple of vacations should give you a clue as to how long he's been a bachelor. If he was with a gang of guys both times, chances are you're the first lady in his life for a while. If, however, he vacationed with a girlfriend the last couple of times, he'll probably mention her. Ask about his apartment and he'll probably let on what kind of neighborhood it's in (handy for guessing how much money he earns) and whether he lives alone or with a roommate (which will at least let you know whether you can straddle him over the kitchen table without worrying about being interrupted).

Volunteer roughly the same amount of information about yourself as he gives you about himself. If he goes home from the date having volunteered his star sign, blood type and the inseam measurement for his pants and doesn't even know where you grew up, he'll feel a bit exposed. A date where one party knows all about the other one but not vice versa has not been a success.

Think of the way you expose information about yourself as a striptease—men hit titty bars to see lapdancers peel their clothes off slowly and seductively, revealing an inch at a time. They wouldn't pay to see a stripper who's out of her clothes in five seconds flat.

Answer any questions he has for you, but try not to hog the conversation. I know that this is easier said than done, especially when we're nervous and out to impress. Our natural reaction under such circumstances is to turn any conversation around to the subject of ME ME ME. For example, he tells you that last week he went to Tokyo on a business trip last week. The best answer to that would be, "I was there last year. What'd you think of it?"—thus, you've set the scene for an exchange of experiences and views that's evenly balanced. Instead, if you launch into a ten-minute account of the time you got wasted on sake in the Roppongi district and ended up in a bar full of male escorts, he won't want to volunteer information if he thinks you're going to turn the conversation back around to yourself the whole time. Extend this from your conversation into your body language. Forget what you look like. Don't be vain. Don't let him see you reapply your lipstick. Men do not find this attractive yet you find women doing it at the dinner table. Would you brush your hair there?

To stop you from droning on about yourself, concentrate on listening rather than talking. Waiting a beat before answering makes you look like you've really considered the question. If he keeps clearing his throat, it's a sign he's using that as a two-second delay to think about what he's saying to you, to make sure he says the right thing. He's out to impress and he likes you!

Another cunning tactic to make him feel at ease is to paraphrase what he's said. Re-arrange his words to summarize his last paraphrase. It makes him feel you've really understood and you're really listening. "I see, so you're saying that…" or, "I can't believe you…." It also keeps the conversation from drying up. Better to repeat yourselves a little than be plagued by awkward silences.

Sometimes no matter how hard you try, the chat dries up. When there's a lull in conversation, it's only natural to search our brains frantically for something new to talk about. This is fine in theory, but in practice we'll always come up with something at best irrelevant and, at worst, plain weird.

Random, desperate attempts at reviving the conversation à la "I don't know about you, but I'll never get over losing Elvis" will just throw him off guard. Instead, chill things out by going back over old ground, even if it's only reminiscing about things that happened the night you met, or five minutes ago when the lisping waiter made you both laugh.

Don't be too eager to please. Agreeing with everything he says won't impress him—he'll just think you don't have any opinions of your own, and you could regret it later. Nodding your head and saying "I think so, too" when he extols the virtues of Ozzy Osbourne's early records is all very well when you want to impress him early on, but it'll bite you on the ass later on when he makes you listen to the god-damned tunes. Then again, try not to let small talk turn into a heated debate. Obviously, if he says something that's never going to be accept-able to you (racist comments, sexist remarks, homophobic ignorance), make that clear and let his opinions play a part in whether you choose to see him again or not. But if there's a more minor difference of opin-ion that you don't want to back down on, say, "Let's agree to disagree, otherwise it'll be the end of a beautiful friendship." This lets him know you're not dumbing down or acceding his point of view, but that you're enjoying his company and want to keep the evening nice.

subjects to avoid

Don't complain about your work problems. It's a real turn-off—think how you'd feel if this fabulous, charming man was completely absorbed in the way those stupid bastards in the finance department have cut his yearly paperclip allowance by a third.

Don't complain about your personal problems—a strong, together woman will appeal to him far more than a whiny, needy one. He's not ready to be your emotional support just yet. That's what your friends are for.

Don't ask why he's single. By all means listen if he volunteers that information, but it might be a sensitive subject. It also sounds as though you're looking for faults rather than curious to discover his good points.

Don't talk about your past sexploits. He might be imagining what it would be like to have sex up a tree with you, but he doesn't want to know that that's just normal first date behavior as far as you're concerned.

Don't talk about recent dates or dating disasters—if these other men didn't want to see you again, why should he? In fact, give away as little as possible about what you're looking for, relationship-wise. It's too early for that.

Don't mention the words "love" or "marriage" or talk about how many children you want. You'll look like a sperm bandit—a woman who just wants a man, any man. And he'll run a mile.

But by the same token, don't appear too cool. I've often made the mistake of being so eager not to look desperate that I virtually started the date with a statement about how I wasn't looking for anything serious just yet and repeatedly throwing casual asides in about how much I valued my independence. Then I'd go home and be devastated when he didn't call. You'd be surprised how many of us make this mistake.

Don't witter on about yourself.

If you told any white lies to impress him while you were hitting on him, now's the time to get them out of the way, before your little while lie becomes a big black cloud. When I was a cash-strapped work-experience student still living at home, I told a potential boyfriend that my dad was my roommate because I was too ashamed to admit I didn't have my own place and had to backtrack furiously when the guy became a boyfriend and actually came over. The best way to deal with this is to simply say, "I have a confession to make" and then top it off with a flirty "Well, I knew I had to get to know you by hook or by crook!"

when bad dates happen to good people

Sometimes, no matter how much you want it to, a date isn't going well and you know you don't want to take things any further. This could be for a variety of reasons. Perhaps he's expressing some views that make you really uncomfortable. Perhaps you don't like the way he's been talking to your tits all night. Maybe he's incredibly dull. Maybe, when viewed without your beer goggles, he looks like Shrek. Whatever. Sometimes, you just know it's not going to work.

There are certain circumstances in which an abrupt departure is allowed. Say he's drunk, rude and boorish and really embarrassing you or scaring you. If you're extremely uncomfortable and worried you're putting your personal safety at risk, feel free to ask the maitre d', barman or doorman to call you a cab and excuse yourself by simply saying to your date, "I don't think this is going to work. Thanks for the drink/dinner/movie, but I really want to go home now." Life's too short to sit still and endure a date from hell just because you're too embarrassed to do anything about it. It's better to feel awkward for this one moment than to expend your finite mortality on a creepoid.

However, climbing out of a window, absconding while he's in the restroom or walking out is only permissible if your date is turning out to be a really nasty piece of work (and pretty much guaranteed to split the seams of your sleek pencil skirt and put runs in your $20 tights). If his offense is minor—say, he's just dull, or he doesn't like the same authors as you, or he has a side part—but he's a decent guy, then you owe it to him to at least let him down with his dignity intact.

You know by now that you should always have a friend to call you to check you're safe. Make sure you have an emergency escape plan that this friend is fully aware of so that if things aren't going well you can always pretend she's gone into labor/has locked herself out of your apartment/is in the police station having been wrongly arrested for dealing crack and desperately needs your help NOW. Yes, this is cowardly and unfair, but it saves both of you the embarrassment of having to admit that you're not hitting it off face to face— the harsh words can be said over the phone at a later date.

who pays?

The issue of who pays on a first date is still a bit of a social hot potato. Handled wrong, it can be awkward and embarrassing. Handled right, however, it needn't be an issue at all. It used to be a given that the man would always pay for the lady, but that was back in the dark ages when it used to be a given that the man always earned more. Now that women's earnings are almost on par with—and in some cases far outstrip—their male counterparts, we need some new rules.

As a general rule, whoever asked for the date should foot the bill. Notable exceptions to this rule are if one of you is much, much richer

EAT, DRINK—BUT DON'T BE TOO MERRY

Fact: We can't metabolize alcohol as fast as men can, so no matter how tempted you are to sink beer after beer, don't match your date drink for drink. This is easier said than done when you're nervous, but it's better to have butterflies in your stomach than puke all over your shoes.

A lot of bars serve spirits in double measures as a matter of course—it's worth glancing at the bottles behind the bar and checking out the optic measures so you can keep track of how much you're putting away. If you're taking turns going to the bar, order yourself a soft (or at least weak) drink every time it's your round. He need never know.

Getting drunk on an empty stomach is a really bad idea. If you're going out for dinner, eat a couple of slices of toast before you head out. Not only is bread excellent for soaking up the booze, it'll also keep you from gorging during your main meal.

than the other. If, for example, you're a futures broker with a six-figure salary romancing a penniless struggling actor, it's just silly to expect him to fork out for your bruschetta. Many men are still uncomfortable about the idea of a woman picking up the tab, however, and you don't want him to sit through the date stressing about how he's going to afford this next bottle of Laurent Perrier champagne, so make it clear in advance that tonight is your treat. If his pride is wounded, soften the blow by telling him you'll let him pay next time. That evens the score as well as tells him you're interested in seeing him again.

If he insists on paying, he might be an old-fashioned traditionalist, and it's up to you whether this is a good thing in a boyfriend or not. When up against the kind of guy who's determined not to let me part with any cash, I personally always at least offer to go halves. If he refuses to take the cash I'm about to pull out of my purse, I accept graciously with a "Well, if you're sure, thank you very much," and, if I want to repeat the experience, use the line about letting it be my treat next time.

If you want to go Dutch, then split the bill evenly down the middle, regardless of who ate what, even if you had soup and a salad and he had the lobster thermidore followed by chateaubriand steak. Always have a few small bills ready for the tip—15 percent should do it, so carry some single bills in your purse for this occasion. If he quibbles about who ate what to the nearest penny and doesn't want to leave a tip—even on a first date where he's desperate to impress—then he's either poverty stricken, in which case you might want to think about whether you can handle that long-term, or he's a tight-fisted, anally retentive loser. Don't ignore either of these warning signs.

If the issue of who's paying for whom still hasn't been cleared up by the time the bill comes, it's totally unacceptable for you to skulk off to the toilet to powder your nose when it arrives, or look embarrassed and avoid eye contact until he has to pull out his credit card. I can't stress how important it is to be upfront and not resort to lame girly tactics that put us back ten years. If it's not clear where things stand, he's probably as confused as you are, and if you're the first one to be direct and ask "What shall we do about the bill?" he'll be relieved that you cleared the air.

If the upshot of all this is that he does want to treat you, remember your manners and say "Thank you." Then, and only then, you may take this opportunity to do a quick spot check for spinach on your teeth / pasta sauce on your chin.

at the end of the date

best case scenario

If you enjoyed yourself, say so. Not only is it impeccably good manners, but it also gives him the opportunity to let you know he had fun as well. You've taken the fear of rejection away from him, which makes him more likely to reciprocate genuinely, positively and not play it too cool. If things are going well, now is an excellent time to say whether you'd like to see each other again. A simple "We must do that again sometime" should be all the encouragement he needs to suggest a second date. If he does ask you again, it still doesn't pay to be too available, so make sure you're unable to meet him for at least the following two days. This might take a lot of willpower if the thought of him strutting around your bedroom wearing nothing but a smile has had you salivating all evening, but remember the old showbiz motto: "Always leave 'em wanting more." It's a far safer bet to let your absence make his heart (not to mention what's behind his zipper) grow fonder for a couple of days.

worst case scenario

If you're trying to dump him, don't pussyfoot around with silly lines and subtle hints. Sure, our friends would translate "You'll make someone a wonderful boyfriend one day" as "Get lost, loser" in a millisecond, but he is a man so will translate it simply as "You're wonderful." Guys, when receiving bad news, need to be told with plenty of eye contact and in no uncertain terms. Just say, "I've had a really nice evening, but I can't see us ever being anything more than friends. But I would like to keep in touch with you." This will soften the blow without leaving too much room for confusion. Why should you keep in touch with a man you don't like? Networking, sweetie! If his lifestyle appealed to you, chances are he has some interesting single friends, he knows some people who could further your career, or he'd be perfect for one of your friends.

Don't dismiss this last possibility completely: My closest male friend, Tim, spent the best part of a year chasing Mia, a girl who didn't really like him but was too polite to say so outright. Instead, after a couple of disastrous dates, she casually mentioned that he'd hit it off really well with a friend of hers named Bonnie. His first reaction was that he must be the worst kisser in the history of the world, ever, and that Mia was just making excuses not to see him again. But, true to her word, Mia arranged to turn up to a concert where she knew Tim would be and brought her friend Bonnie with her. Tim and Bonnie locked eyes across a sweaty dance floor and we haven't been able to pry them apart since.

Obviously, it's only worthwhile trying to salvage a friendship with your date if all that was missing was sexual chemistry or that X factor that makes two people really click. If he's a creepy little slug with no redeeming qualities, then just hope that this town is big enough for the two of you and that you manage to live out the rest of your days without bumping into him again.

kiss me, you fool!

The end-of-date kiss is a big deal, whether you've kissed before or not. I personally work on the principle that you should kiss every frog you can because you never know which of them will turn into a prince. This is a secret I have known since my late teens when, out of boredom, I made out with a boy my friends and I had previously known as Crusty Kev. He wasn't much to look at, but when his lips touched mine, it was almost an out-of-body experience. If you have any desire whatsoever to kiss him, do it. You never know which men have the capacity to bring you pleasure beyond imagination.

Who makes the first move? The natural progression of things on a date means that often there's no such thing as a "first move," but rather the physical tension builds slowly throughout the date and the kiss is a natural progression from there. If you know for sure a kiss is coming (e.g., he's been stroking your knee all evening and saying things like "I can't wait to kiss you"), it's totally easy to make it happen. Just nuzzle into his neck and tilt your face towards his, stop talking and smile. If he seems shy, or you haven't kissed yet and you're still at the plutonic stage but you want to get physical, try this. Take his face in your hands and give him a light lip kiss that lingers. This is very sexy and, while it's not actually going for the kiss proper (nothing short of forcing his lips apart with your tongue is actually going for the kiss proper), it will leave him in no doubt as to your naughty intentions.

Certain situations are more conducive to kissing than others. Leaning across dinner tables in chic restaurants isn't advisable, nor is pawing away at the bar. But snugly booths or alcoves in clubs, tops of buses, any kind of line are great moments to go for it. Low lighting is your friend. It's worth bearing in mind that the more public the kiss, the more time you have to decide whether you want to follow it up; it's easier to decide whether or not you want to go home and have sex with him than it is if you kiss for the first time on his doorstep.

Cabs are excellent places to kiss, not least because the bright lights of the big city flashing by as you speed home are an exciting aphrodisiac in themselves. Caveat: lock lips at the taxi stand, rather than in the taxi itself. It's vital to establish whether or not there is sexual chemistry before deciding where you're going home to. Picture the scene: Your date in a downtown bar was a success. You haven't kissed yet but you hit it off really well. Even though you live on opposite sides of town, you agree to go back to his place for coffee. In the cab, he closes his eyes and his lips bear down on yours. It's like French kissing a washing machine. It's vile. Not only do you have to make your excuses and leave, but you also have to fork out $20 for a cab ride all the way across town, money you could've spent on a really nice pair of silk panties!

Think of sex as the pot of gold at the end of your dating rainbow—getting there was a beautiful and colorful journey, but this is what you really came for. It's time to show him just why you put the Sex into Sexy Bitch.

There are a million things that can be said about sex with a long-term partner, but first-night sex is a whole 'nother ballgame, and this is all you need to get by without it being a nightmare. Worrying about whether you're really making an emotional connection or reaching the one-hour orgasm you read about in *Cosmo* is for when you have a proper boyfriend. Tonight, you're faced with a very different set of concerns. Namely, what will I look like, how do I make the first move, which position should I do it in and who's going to be the first one to say the word "condom."

The trick is to plan ahead for any potential passion pitfalls. This will take away the source of your worries, leaving you free to actually go on and enjoy the beauty and deliciousness of the physical act of love. Go for it, tiger!

when should you have sex with him?

Of course, in a totally liberated world, when you slept with a guy wouldn't have any bearing on what he thought of you or how it affected your subsequent relationship. But then again, in a totally perfect world, high heels would be retractable so you could run for the bus when you needed to. Opinion on whether you should wait differs from man to man. Many men think that nice girls make them wait before putting out, while some men want to have sex as soon as possible and don't see why two people who obviously like each other should cool their passions because of an outdated moral code. Women's opinions are just as varied. Some girls need to feel they've made a real connection with the man in question before they can get genuinely physically turned on, and have to have known him for a good few weeks before they can trust him enough to relax in bed. Others think it's pointless prolonging the moment—after all, if you've given up three nights of your life to get to know a man, only to find that you're utterly incompatible between the sheets, it can be quite annoying.

If all you want from this particular guy is a night of physical pleasure beyond imagination, then by all means don't waste three or four dates on him. Take him home there and then, give him the time of his life, say a fond but firm farewell in the morning, and don't let anyone tell you that it makes you a bad person. One-night stands have their advantages: You're free to be as wild as you like, you don't have to try too hard to impress some guy you'll probably never see again, you can be selfish, and you will almost always pick up a couple of handy new moves.

But if he's someone you really want to make into your boyfriend, it won't do any harm to make him wait a little while. After all, if you'll drop your drawers as soon as you make eye contact with a man across a bar, it doesn't make him feel very special. Delay the action a little bit and he'll think it was his charm and magnetism that burrowed away at you until you were finally ready to surrender yourself to him. Men aren't above playing mind games to establish where we stand. One otherwise chivalrous male friend of mine confesses to trying it with every girl on the first date in the hope she'll say no and make him work a little harder for it. I would have been really angry with him if I hadn't been so impressed at the fact a man had managed to employ even that small degree of cunning in the first place. (Placing so much importance on the thrill of the chase is a pretty neanderthal attitude, but that's because it's an evolutionary leftover from when he *was* a caveman and hunter, so try not to hold it against him too much.)

The fact that you saw him first, made the effort to find out about him, turned up at a party you knew he'd be at and then stealthily flirted with him until he had no choice but to approach you does not affect the way he feels about this. In fact, if you've spun your web of seduction carefully and correctly, he won't even realize he's the fly, not the spider. He certainly won't respect you less, and the anticipation will have both of you hornier than hell by the time you do finally get around to playing hide the sausage.

Making him wait a little while has other advantages besides letting your mutual libidos build to a soaring crescendo. It also gives you time to do your bikini line, tidy up your bedroom, buy some new underwear and run through the event in your head in gloriously naughty detail. Not to mention calling your friends to ask for pointers.

If he tries to bully you into sex, don't give him the time of day because it's a sign of how he's going to treat you in the future. If he can't show a little patience and understanding at this stage, what's he going to be like a couple of months down the line when he's not on his best behavior? My friend Kelly can vouch for this: Warning bells should have chimed for her when an old boyfriend refused to schedule a first date for a week she had her period (and no, I don't know how that conversation came about). Sure enough, it turned out that he was just using her for sex—although he was kind enough to give her a break from screwing him when his real girlfriend came home from college in Miami.

Don't ever feel you owe him anything. A wise man-friend of mine once told me that he hates it when women go out thinking men expect sex as their right. "We certainly don't expect it but we hope for it," he said. If you really don't want to have sex with a man, make sure you go home separately. This way, if he's a nice guy, you won't be giving out any mixed messages that confuse him and make him wonder if he's got BO. And if he's a nasty number, you're doing yourself a favor by getting out of a potentially risky situation.

your place or mine?

Unless you've got something to hide—a hideous, grungy apartment, awful roommates or indeed a husband and five children in which case shame on you, it's a good idea to invite him back to your place. Statistically, you're safer in your own home than going to someone else's, especially if you don't know him that well (don't you just hate it when you go home with that lovely clean-cut young man, only to find he's converted his bedroom into a dungeon? I know I do).

The advantages of being on your territory don't end there. You have access to all your own products so you can take off your own make-up without having to resort to scraping off your upper epidermis with a tissue and some ancient after-shave balm. You know how to find the bathroom in the middle of the night, which negates the possibility of going through the wrong door and crawling into bed with his roommate by mistake at three in the morning, AND you can deck the bedroom out in lots of teensy, tiny fairy lights that will create an instant "soft focus" effect on your skin, disguising cellulite and pasty skin as if by magic.

If you do go to his place, make a note of where it is—not least because it's scary enough waking up with someone for the first time without the added worry of not knowing which zipcode you're in. Call or text-message a friend to let them know where you are—and let him see you doing it. Explain that you and your friends make it a rule to look out for each other. If he's a gentleman, he'll understand.

that condom question

Unless you both have a clean bill of sexual health, there really is no question—you must use condoms. I know I'm pretty much preaching to the choir here and that, as a sexy bitch, you take your sexual health pretty seriously. But I can't stress enough how important it is that you take responsibility for your own protection when you're dating. I know you know perfectly well that condoms are the most effective way to protect you from pregnancy and a whole host of icky diseases that will at best give you an unpleasant itching sensation in your crotch and at worst kill you. But research shows that at least half of us don't use condoms with a new partner because we're simply too damned embarrassed to know how to go about it.

Even sexy bitches are sometimes ashamed to carry condoms in the first place because—they reckon—men think that girls who carry condoms are sluts. Hmm. Maybe for our mothers' generation, but today's man about town is more likely to be relieved than appalled on hearing that his date has brought her own protection. Again, never underestimate how lazy men are—he's more likely to think of a condom-carrying girl in terms of the trip to the drugstore she's saved him than what a tart she is.

And—and this is the really stupid part—even those of us who always have a condom tucked away in our handbags often don't use them because we can't find the words to bring up the subject, or we think it'll kill the moment. I say, if you know him well enough to sit on his penis, you know him well enough to talk about condoms.

Just ask him, "Do you have any protection?" He'll know exactly what you mean, but you don't have to say the word "condom" if that's what's freaking you out (why is condom such an ugly word? Why?). Act as if it's a given that you use condoms and he'll be unlikely to question it. And if he does offer you flimsy excuses, he's a jerk and doesn't deserve to have sex with you in the first place.

Popular flimsy excuses are "But I won't be able to feel anything," which isn't true. He might be slightly desensitized, but look on the bright side: that means he'll last a little longer than usual and won't pop his cork prematurely. Even the longest-lasting lover can find he comes a little quicker when he's having sex with a new woman for the first time. He might try "I can't get condoms big enough for me" (or indeed, "I can't get condoms small enough for me"). If that's the case, it should be up to him to buy condoms in a size that accommodates him comfortably, but it's worth having a variety stashed in your bedside drawer just in case. He might try "I'm allergic to latex," and this could be true, but if it is, again, it's his responsibility to carry non-latex or lambskin condoms with him whenever he thinks he might get lucky. And you're perfectly entitled to tell him this, too.

If you do have a variety pack stashed in your bedside drawer, don't let him see the whole box. The sight of 24 different condoms all at once will get him thinking. His first reaction will probably be "How many times does she expect me to perform tonight?" Then he'll move onto wondering just how many men you bring home with you—he doesn't want to think of himself as just another notch on your bedpost any more than you want to think of yourself as just one in a long line of his conquests. There's a difference, in a guy's mind, between a girl who buys a packet of three specifically because she wants to sleep with *him* and a girl who's permanently on standby.

If you're worried about spoiling the moment, tear off the corner of the condom packet when you're pretty worked up and it's obvious you're going to have sex soon but you're not quite ready for penetration. This tear will make the process smoother and easier when the moment comes—neither of you is going to be aroused by the sight of the other person turning red in the face while they struggle with the perforations at the corner of the packet. Just don't leave the opened packet longer than five minutes in case the condom's built-in lubrication dries out.

No matter how tough it is to open the condom, don't attempt to tear it out with your teeth. It might look sexy, wanton and extravagant, but the last thing you want is a rip in the rubber. Likewise, try not to get any body lotion, oil or make-up on the condom because it doesn't take much to dissolve the latex, and make sure your condom conforms to U.S. safety standards by checking for the mark that means it's been tried and tested (don't ask me how). Novelty rubbers often don't carry this mark, so beware the Blueberry Tickler you bought in the club vending machine. It might look hilarious and even feel quite good, but there's no guarantee it'll protect you.

Hold the condom by the little teat at the end (this is going to catch his drift, if you catch my drift) and put it on the tip of the penis. Use your other hand to roll the condom all the way down until the base of the condom is about level with his balls. You do need to concentrate pretty hard on getting this right, but add a couple of gasps and he'll think you're staring at his totem pole in rapt adoration rather than squinting to check it's on properly. Once he's wearing the condom, stroke it downward firmly a couple of times, partly to make sure it's nice and snug and partly for fun.

all mouth and no pants

For a sex trick that means you'll go down (pun intended) as the lay of his life, or to persuade a reluctant guy to wear a condom, learn how to put it on him using your mouth. Do it right, and it'll feel amazing for him, as well as give him something interesting to watch. Look mom, no hands!

Don't forget to wipe your mouth clean of all make-up first as even a slick of lip-balm can dissolve the rubber of the condom. (Body oils, massage balms, hand lotions and pretty much any moisturizer can also wreck the rubber, so if you're rubbing him down with baby oil before sex, make sure you towel all traces of the slippery stuff off your bodies and hands before using the condom). Use a flavored condom because a mouthful of untreated rubber isn't the best taste in the world, and keep a glass of fruit juice by the bed to freshen up your mouth before you resume kissing.

Cover your teeth with your lips so you don't tear the condom and use light suction to hold the teat of the condom between your lips. You might be tempted to laugh, especially if you catch sight of yourself in a mirror at this crucial point, but try to compose your features into an expression of rapt adoration, as though you can't imagine anything you'd rather be doing. Visualizing a chocolate eclair often helps at this point. Slowly bear down on his erection, using your tongue and lips to push it all the way down. Use the fingers of one hand to help if you need to and, when you're sure it's on snug, use both hands to smooth it down. Do the rapt adoration thing one more time, and hop on.

You probably won't get this right the first time, so if you want a little practice, wait until you're sure you're on your own (roommates out of the country, curtains drawn, phone off the hook, etc.) and practice on a dildo, a cucumber or something else vaguely the shape and size of the human male appendage. You'll soon be an old hand at it. Or is that an old mouth?

strip tips from the professionals

Taking your clothes off in front of a new man for the first time is one of the most nerve-wracking experiences a woman can have. If you're not worrying about his reaction when he sees your naked body for the first time, you're wondering whether pulling your top over your head will smudge your make-up or if you remembered to put your nice underwear on.

As with every aspect of the dating game, preparation is key. I recommend having an undressing rehearsal to see if it's easy for your chosen outfit to be slipped out of seductively—nothing kills the mood of love faster than lying down on your back and getting him to pull your ankles because it's the only way you can get out of your black tapered satin trousers. I know what I'm talking about here. My first ever magazine job involved auditioning to be a lapdancer at a topless bar and I took to the stage in a layered black chiffon dress with a deep V neckline and little floaty sleeves. It was a rather elegant little number even if I do say so myself. However, up on the podium, it was a different story—when it came to the moment of truth, the other girls undid the spaghetti straps that were holding their dresses up with an imperceptible flick of their fingers, while I was left staggering around on the stage unable to see anything because my unstretchy dress got stuck over my head. By the time I did get out of it, the other girls were pirouetting around a pole in their panties and I was left on stage wearing little else other than a blush that started at my cheeks and covered most of my upper body.

Unsurprisingly, I didn't get the gig. But I did pick up some tips on how to undress to impress. The following information is based on a very interesting conversation I had with a pair of lapdancers at that audition. The advice they gave me has been toned down a little here for those of you without a fireman's pole in your boudoir, or, indeed, the perfect body of a lapdancer.

Undressing for sex tends to follow one of the following two patterns: either you coyly agree to go upstairs and disrobe shyly in front of each other, or you rip each other's clothes off on the sofa. You really want to try to achieve a happy medium between the two—shyly undressing each other on the sofa, say.

You can do it as slowly or as quickly as you want. There are no rules that say you have to slide your hand under your bra to play with your own nipples while you sashay to "Justify My Love." I mean, feel free to do it if you want, but unless you're both drunk as skunks, it'll be like you're having a competition to see who can feel the most embarrassed.

First things first—shoes. This is where those four-inch ankle-snappers finally come into their own. The way you take your shoes off can be used as an indicator of how you're going to be in bed. With first-night sex, take them off first. Kicking a stiletto across the room makes you look like the kind of girl who's going to leap into everything with gay abandon. Likewise, sitting on the edge of the bed and taking a long, long time to unzip a knee-high boot says you're cool, calm and very much in control. Drawing any kind of attention to a high-heeled shoe is foxy. Bending down to undo the Velcro on your sneakers is less so. If you think your shoes are going to be a problem, try to slip them off surreptitiously earlier on in the evening.

Make sure you're totally aware of all buttons and zips, hooks and eyes, laces and ribbons that keep you in your clothes. If you can maintain eye contact with him as you slowly unbutton your slinky top, you'll achieve the desired effect of reducing him to a quivering wreck of lust. Scowling at a stuck zipper and swearing as you tug at it will just reduce him to a quivering wreck of laughter.

Skirts should be slid down the hips and then slipped out of. Slide pants slowly down over your hips and then step out of them one leg at a time. If you haven't taken your shoes off first, you'll find that your pants get stuck at the ankles, leaving your dignity conspicuous by its absence.

If you have a dress on, step OUT of it if you possibly can. If you HAVE to take it off over your head, cross your arms and whip it off in one swift move—practice until you can do this smoothly. The effect you're going for is similar to a magician who can whip off a tablecloth without disturbing the 50-piece china tea set on the table.

Taking off the bra is the moment he's been waiting for, which is why most of us get so nervous. Petite ladies worry that he'll whip out his magnifying glass the minute he realizes a Wonderbra has been making mountains out of molehills, and well-endowed women panic that he'll head for the hills when he sees the way their breasts head for the floor without their minimizer. Well, I have some good news for you—by now, your breasts are going to look beautiful to him because he's about to have sex. Fact. To undress your breasts, unhook your bra yourself from the back and let it fall to the floor, or, if you're going for the gay abandon angle, fling it across the room so it lands on a lamp-shade/picture frame/the cat. Then stretch your arms up or, if you're leaving your bra on until the very last possible moment, immediately assume the sexual position that flatters your particular breast type (see below).

Pantyhose vs. stockings: Hose are lovely and comfy but are pretty much impossible to wriggle out of with any degree of sexiness, no matter how perfect your body. They're also a little unhygienic and unkind to your private parts. Do you really want to offer him a crotch that's been sweating in nylon for the past four hours? Garters, on the other hand, say that you're the kind of sophisticated, high-maintenance lady who demands nothing but the best—and that includes him. If you're wearing stockings and a garter belt, make sure you put your panties on over them—not only will this making going to the bathroom a lot easier over the course of the evening, it also gives you the option of slipping your underwear off over your stockings and garter belt and leaving them on during sex. If you want to get completely naked, unhook your garters one by one before rolling each stocking down your leg, pulling it off over your foot and letting the stocking fall to the floor. Elastic-band knee- or thigh-highs can also be removed via the roll-down and fall method, but don't say I didn't warn you about stocking scarring (see "Legs," below).

If you're lucky, he'll be slowly peeling off your panties with his teeth by now, but if you'd rather remove your own underwear, then hook your thumbs in the front and peek down seductively, look up and make eye contact with him, then slide them down slowly before stepping out of them one leg at a time. Obviously, this works best if you're not wearing industrial-strength control-top tummy tuckers.

unzipping your man

Learning how to undress him with confidence is almost more important than how you disrobe. He'll love you for it, not least because few women are ballsy enough to take off a new partner's clothes firmly and decisively. Taking his clothes off for him gives the impression you're confident and in charge, and helps you set the pace—you can rip his shirt off him and let the buttons fly if you're in the mood for fast, furious sex. Likewise, lingering over every button and every zip sets the scene for slow, sensual, touchy-feely lovemaking.

Don't be tempted to dive straight into his pants—start with his top layer and make him wait for his below-the-belt action. Again, delayed gratification is far more rewarding than instant access. If he's wearing a T-shirt or something else that doesn't button, slide your hands up around his chest, during which time you may or may not want to comment on the gorgeous manliness of his pectoral muscles. While your groping hands are up there, simply slide his top off over his head.

A lot of men love it when a lady makes a beeline for the penis, as though she can't wait to sample the goods. So don't give him the satisfaction—make him wait before you whip out his willy, always making it the last bit of him you reveal.

Never try and pull a penis out through a man's fly or the hole in the front of his boxers. Even they struggle with this and they've had plenty of practice, doing it several times a day whenever they go for a pee. Instead, make sure you undo his fly first (again, control the pace to tease or thrill him, depending on what you're going for) and thank your lucky stars if he's got a button fly. I await the day when Levi's 501s enjoy a fashion revival because unzipping a man always carries the risk of putting him out of action for the rest of the month, let alone the evening. When you get to his boxers, pull the waistband out and let his erection peek over the top of his shorts for one tantalizing moment, then slowly slide them off. Don't forget to look impressed. Penises are like Christmas presents: You're allowed to feel through the wrapping and guess what's inside, but you still have to compose your facial features into an expression of delight even if it's not quite what you were hoping Santa was going to bring you.

sex positions that flatter your figure

So you're naked and fooling around. Sorry to interrupt, but now is not the time to let body insecurities spoil your performance. So with these sex moves to flatten your stomach, slim your thighs and perk up your boobs, you'll never make love in the dark again.

A lot of people reckon good sex starts on the inside: that if you feel good about yourself and worship your own inner goddess, you'll be a great lover. There's a grain of truth in this, but the fact remains that the first time you sleep with someone, no matter how often you repeat the mantra "My soul is beautiful and my innate gorgeousness will shine through," it doesn't work when your butt's a bag of porridge and your sparrow legs make a cocktail stick look shapely.

I think it's much shallower and more simple than that—when you think you look great, you'll be more adventurous in bed, more confident and more relaxed (and the more relaxed you are, the more likely you are to have an orgasm). I also think that for the 99.99 percent of us who weren't blessed with flawless figures, it's perfectly acceptable to cheat.

boobs

My friend Fiona recently lost a lot of weight and, naturally, I hated her with her new jutting collarbone and legs that didn't touch at the top. Until I saw her in a changing room and realized that her once full, glorious breasts were a shrivelled shadow of their former selves. None of us past the age of 16 have perfect tits, but certain positions can allow you to have them. Stretch your arms up above your head to pull the skin on your bust tight; even the heaviest breasts will remain high and mighty. If you're feeling kinky, ask your date to tie you up with a silk stocking (you were listening to me before when I told you to wear stockings, weren't you?).

butt

This isn't what you want to hear, but trust me: The best way to disguise a generous gluteus maximus is to put that derriere in the air and do it doggy style. When you're on all fours, your butt looks smaller and firmer because the skin and muscles are stretched taut. It's doubly sneaky 'cause it flatters your butt but puts it on show at the same time. He'll think you're wonderfully confident about your body, and the view from his end is his idea of heaven. Doggy-style sex is great for bringing out the animal in both of you: your breasts are hanging down so the blood rushes to the nipples, making them even more sensitive to touches and tweaks. If you've already located your G-spot, you'll know that this is a great way for him to reach it. If you haven't, this is a rather fun way to look for it.

Make sure you have a wrap or something on hand if you're self-conscious about letting him see your rear end—nothing screams "I HATE MY BODY" louder than a lady who backs out of the bedroom.

legs

Don't hide chunky calves; make them part of foreplay by dressing them up. Blessed as I am with a pair of legs that makes those of most NFL players look spindly, I know what I'm talking about here. Take him to bed wearing nothing but a pair of knee-high boots (Nine West make fabulous stretchy ones that elongate the stubbiest of legs).

Leather boots have kinky, dominatrix overtones and can unleash desires in you and him you never knew existed.

There are no other leg problems that can't be sorted out by a good pair of black stockings. Plain ones will lengthen and slim down short chunky legs, while skinny legs will benefit from patterned or fishnet stockings in whatever color you feel bold enough to carry off; the patterns will add shape and define every muscle in your legs. If you're lucky enough to have the thighs of a gazelle, you can get away with lace-top thigh-highs. The rest of us (i.e., pretty much everyone old enough to have left school) should stick to garters unless we're feeling confident enough to deal with the unsightly overspill and red welts when we finally take the stockings off.

feet

There are no such things as beautiful or ugly feet, just good and bad pedicures.

thighs

Smooth out flabby thighs by lying back and stretching your legs as far back over your head as you can manage. This will flex your hamstrings and disguise cellulite, working much on the same principle as the butt-flattering position described above. It's also a surprisingly comfortable position to have sex in, allowing easy penetration and thrusting for him, and great clitoral stimulation. If you're worried about cellulite, take a tip from Hollywood actresses and make sure you're well-lit. Lighting from above casts a shadow, making your skin look lumpier. Low-level lighting is softer and much more flattering. Try fairylights, tea lights around the floor, or a lamp at the same height as the bed.

skinny rib?

If you're skinny all over and feel you lack feminine curves, make the most of your light-as-a-feather body and just show off, dammit. He lies on his back and you lie on your back, on top of him, easing yourself down onto his erection. It's pretty energetic but you don't actually have to do much because he plays with your boobs and your clitoris, and all you have to do to get intense G-spot pressure is to lean further back against his body.

tummy

I recently read the following in an interview with Britney Spears' personal trainer: "Britney's so dedicated. Whenever she's got a spare minute, she's on the floor doing stomach crunches." Obviously, girls with real jobs, real lives and sex to be had can think of a million other ways to spend their free time, which is why very few of us have concave Britney-esque stomachs. Which is where a little strategic positioning comes in handy. While in the missionary position, the flesh on your stomach falls back and to the sides, making it look flatter. But be warned: one false move—like rolling on to your side or bending in half and any little rolls of fat will be magnified. But it is possible to hide pot bellies and saggy tummies without lacing yourself into a rib-crushing corset (although if that's what turns you on, who am I to stop you?). Instead, bend over, put that glorious booty of yours in the air, lean over a handy piece of furniture (the edge of a bed or sofa, or the kitchen counter, for example), look kittenishly over your shoulder and invite him to take you from behind. I predict this is one invitation he'll RSVP to and come. This is the stuff of male fantasies—he'll be so busy thinking what a great lay you are, the last thing on his mind will be your tummy that's currently squished. Keep him thinking you're a wonderfully in-control lover by asking him to play with your clitoris. Not only will this be delicious for you, it also keeps his busy hands from wandering north and finding your love handles!

sex positions for him

It obviously takes time to get to know a new man's body and what turns it on and off, but in the meantime, get busy with these positions that accommodate his own physical imperfections.

if he's heavy

There's nothing more uncomfortable than being stuck beneath a 200-pound quarterback during sex (or so I've heard). He needs to prop himself up on his arms if he's on top, but if you're feeling frisky, straddle him and ride him like a cowgirl in a rodeo. It's great if you want to feel in control, it's a huge visual treat for him and he doesn't have to put much effort into it. Which, if he's the kind of couch potato who's let himself get flabby, he'll probably appreciate.

if he's over-endowed

If he's the kind of guy who could use a third pantsleg, you could be in for the time of your life. However, sex with an outsized penis can be uncomfortable and have you shifting around to avoid his turbo thrusts until you're squatting on the pillow wearing your earrings as ankles. If your date turns out to be a too-big boy, try spooning from behind: you lie on your side and he snuggles into your back and slides his penis between your legs and inside you. You'll both have a limited range of movement so he can't do that deep thrusting thing, and besides, it's nice and cuddly.

if he's under-endowed

My own jury's still out over whether size matters: While it needs to at least touch the sides, I reckon an inventive, attentive lover can more than make up for a teeny tail. And the good news is that men who aren't very big usually know about it and overcompensate by being wonderfully skilled. If he's on top, pull your legs in towards your chest; this squeezes him inside you so it feels like a much tighter fit. But the best bet is good old doggy style, offering really deep penetration. So who'd have thought it? A girl with a big butt and a guy with a little dick are a match made in sex heaven!

if he's skinny

So he slips out of his well-cut suit and expensive shirt to reveal a pair of legs that barely support his weight and ribs you could play the xylophone on. But a skinny guy can refresh parts other men can't reach and go all night in the CAT position—the coital alignment technique to you and me. It's a totally new approach to intercourse based on pressure and rocking motions rather than thrusting. He gets on top of you, aligning his pelvis over yours, you wrap your legs around his and he rests on you, and you slowly rock your way to orgasm. With big guys, you often feel like you're suffocating in someone's armpit as he stays on top of you; with Mr. Skinny, you have the freedom to lie back and enjoy yourself.

7 the morning after and beyond

the morning after

Whether you've woken up with a god or a monster, there's nothing quite like the morning after the night before. In many ways, what you do now is even more make or break than the actual sex itself.

For example, if you spent the night talking, laughing and having the kind of orgasms that meant you had to be peeled off the ceiling, you are (unless you're, like, insane) going to want to prolong the magic as long as possible. There's every chance he'll want to see you again, too, but it won't hurt to follow these guidelines. They vary slightly depending on whether you're at your own place or his, but the basics are the same.

No matter how much earlier than him you wake up, it's bad form to leave a slumbering man in your bed while you go about your daily business (unless, of course, that daily business involves freshening yourself up in the bathroom so that you can slip back between the sheets clean, sleek and smelling of frangipani, or whatever other scent you'd like him to believe your armpits naturally exude). It's certainly not OK to leave the house while he's asleep in your bed. Apart from anything else, he might steal your stuff. Men almost never wake up first, which is good because it saves them the sight of us snoring with mouth wide open and drool on the pillow. The correct procedure is to wait until he opens one sleepy eye and smile sweetly at him. All being well, he'll drag you back into his arms there and then, but if he doesn't, it's probably because he's not feeling too daisy-fresh himself.

If he's at your place, offer to make him breakfast or, better still, take him to your local diner for pancakes and coffee. This will eke out the time you have together, it'll get you back on neutral ground and there's nothing like snuggling up in a cafe with the paper to induce a warm fuzzy glow of New Love around the two of you. It's also a sci-entifically proven* fact that there is no better cure for a hangover than high-calorie, high-carb, sugar-laden, diabetes-inducing breakfasts.

If you're at his place, by all means take the opportunity to have a nosy look around his apartment and see what kind of man he really is. Just keep one ear open for the sound of him waking so he doesn't catch you at it.

*In extensive laboratory tests by me and my boyfriend, a plate of syrupy waffles and a bucket of full-fat soda relieve symptoms hang-over remedies like Alka-Seltzer don't even begin to touch.

worst-case scenarios

No matter how well you planned your date (and if you followed my advice to the letter, you should have done it with military pre-cision), there will always be hitches to the perfect morning after. I've anticipated every possible variation on the theme of worst-case scenario here.

I'm smelly and messy!

Bet you wish you'd stayed at your place now, don't you? Your gleaming bathroom with its rows of Clinique cleansers and your very own toothbrush is a world away from his grubby equivalent. Just how *do* boys get by with just one bar of supermarket-brand soap to satisfy all their grooming needs? That said, we'd probably run a mile from any guy who did have eye make-up remover in his bathroom cabinet, right?

If last night's make-up is streaking all over your face, making you look like a particularly tearful member of KISS, don't scrape away at your face with a spit-dampened tissue trying to remove the residue—you'll just redden your skin and look like a tearful version of yourself. Instead, head for his kitchen and grab some cooking oil. Olive oil is best, but if you haven't managed to pick up a gourmand, any kind will do as long as it's vegetable based. Massage a tiny amount of the oil into your face, including your eyes and eyelashes, as you go: the oil will completely remove all traces of the eye make-up and last night's foundation. Now wash your face in his sink using his one lousy bar of soap, taking care to use your fingers to wipe away the oil around your eyes. The soap will remove the oil from your face, but enough will remain to negate the need for a moisturizer. It goes without saying you—don't let him see you do this.

There's nothing like morning breath to put you off a repeat performance, but don't be tempted to use his toothbrush if you forgot your own—there is a teensy chance that you can pick up infections from sharing a toothbrush, and even though you sucked his face and were penetrated by his penis last night, that's no reason to abandon basic hygiene. Instead, use the corner of a towel or washcloth (or even toilet paper) to massage toothpaste into your gums and teeth, then rinse your mouth out with water. Then, and only then, can you slip back into bed with him, fresh of face, fragrant of breath, and loose of morals....

I don't know where I am!

It's more common than you'd think: Even with a man you've known a while, you might not know *exactly* where he lives, and the chances are you weren't looking out of the window much in the taxi back to his place. If you're lucky enough to have gone back to a penthouse on the river with a view of the city landscape, one glance out of the window is enough to get your bearings. But more often than not, one side street or a set of rooftops is pretty indistinguishable from another. You could always ask him, of course, but if you're awake and he's not, it's no fun sitting up in bed and fretting that you could be *anywhere*. So have a sneak around the place. Look for old bank statements (which will happily give you a clue as to how solvent he is) or utility bills (often pinned to the fridge with a novelty magnet if you're out of ideas) with the address clearly printed. This knowledge will at least give you an idea of how long it's going to take you to get home/to work/the hell out. If, for some reason, you have to leave the house still not knowing quite where you are (you're making a quick escape, for example, or he's left you asleep in his bed while he went to work), your best bet is to leave the house and walk in the same direction as everyone else if it's the morning rush hour, or just listen to where the traffic seems to be coming from and hope for the best.

I don't know who he is

This is a very real risk if the gap between meeting this guy and taking him to bed was very short and alcohol had a hand in your behavior. If you're at his place, see above: the house should be awash with clues as to the names of its occupants. Just pray he doesn't have roomies whose names sound a bit like his: checking out the letters on the doorstep and wondering if you've hooked up with Tim or Tom is no fun at all. If he's at your place, you have two options. One, look through his pockets for identifying documentation while he's in the shower. Two, which is less straightforward, find his cell phone, use it to call your cell phone and hope the number shows up, then turn off his phone, call the number and pray that his voicemail message includes his name ("Hi, this is Ben, leave a message" sort of thing rather than "You have reached the mailbox of…"). If none of the above work, simply refer to him as "hot stuff" and hope he's so pleased with the compliment he doesn't notice you don't call him by his name.

I've run out of condoms

That's my girl—your all-night bed-in used up your condom *and* your spare. But if you're still hungry for more, don't be tempted to undo all your good work by having unprotected sex. He should really have some, but if he doesn't, you're going to have to pop to the 7-11 for supplies. Even if you're horny as hell, maybe now's the time to find other ways of getting each other off. There are plenty of places you can accommodate a happy penis other than between your legs, and it's also your chance to find out whether he's an old hand—if you know what I'm saying.

the condom split last night

There's not much you can do at this stage apart from make sure any remaining rubber is well and truly out (a long soak in the bath will speed things along) and get yourself to your doctor or the nearest women's health clinic or Planned Parenthood center ASAP. They will be able to give you a morning-after pill or some other emergency contraception.

lordy—I'm in a hotel

You've scored an out-of-towner so the usual rules don't apply, so take advantage of the fact you don't need to worry about seeing him again, when he's going to call, etc. Chill out, enjoy, soak in the Jacuzzi, watch cable, order room service. On your way out, walk past the concierge, smile and say thank you. Don't worry that they think you're a hooker—hookers rarely stay the night. They'll just think you're a party animal instead. But that's all right.

Trudging home in last night's clothes is a potential walk of shame, but hold your head high enough and look blasé enough and you'll carry it off. If you act as though it's the most normal thing in the world to walk through town wearing a tube top and slinky, low-slung black pleather pants on a Sunday morning, people around you won't question it either. Much.

as bad as it gets

Of course, the *worst* worst-case morning-after scenario is that you've woken up with a man who, without the aid of your beer goggles, is perhaps the ugliest damn thing you ever set eyes on. Actually, simply waking up with him isn't the *worst* worst-case scenario. *Worst* worst-case scenario is waking up when your arm is actually trapped underneath him, making it impossible for you to move without waking him up. This phenomenon is called "coyote arm" because, just as a coyote caught in a trap will gnaw away at his flesh to free the trapped limb, so would you rather chew your arm off and make a clean getaway than face the consequences of waking him. Hence Coyote Ugly.

If the night was a disaster and you don't want to see him again, be as abrupt and businesslike as you can. Don't cuddle him to wake him up. Certainly don't kiss him again, and for god's sake don't have sex with him again. As mercy fucks go, this time you're really doing yourself more harm than good.

If he was a one-night stand, offer him a cup of coffee or a glass of water and offer to show him the way home. This way you're not actually asking him to leave in cold blood, but he should feel sufficiently unwelcome and make his excuses and leave. It's not often in relationships you get the chance to make a clean break, but you can here.

Don't take his number and say you'll call if you don't mean it. Just say "Last night was fun [even if it wasn't] but I don't really want to be seeing anyone right now [even if you do]."

Make up somewhere very important you have to be: a breakfast meeting for work if it's a weekday, a hair appointment on Saturday or church if it's Sunday. Caveat: If you use the work ruse, try to have an idea of where he's headed. If you don't want to see him again, the last thing you want is to be stuck together on the same train or bus. Likewise church.

Sometimes a girl loses interest in a guy she's been seeing for a while as soon as she's slept with him, for any number of reasons.

Maybe you just didn't click in bed, maybe he was kinky and wanted to tie you up and wear a garbage bag on his head during intercourse, or maybe he was a plain old-fashioned bad lay. If you've been dating for a while, the rules are slightly different and you owe him a little sensitivity, not least because he knows where to send the abusive letters and which number to make the obscene phone calls to. No guy likes to be dumped so soon after sex, especially if you've spent a couple of evenings together. He's only human, and he'll feel a little used and abused, not to mention paranoid about his performance. You could set him back years—and even if you think you'd be doing the rest of the women who live in your city a favor by keeping him single and shy, it's not fair to him. Even complete slimeballs have a right to personal development.

if you're at his place

If you're at his place and you can't wait to get away, you have a few options at your disposal. The first, and most obvious, is the Midnight Flit. Don't be fooled by the title—the Midnight Flit refers to any sly getaway perpetrated while you're awake and he's asleep, whether that's by moonlight shadow or dawn's early light. The MF has certain obvious advantages: there are no awkward goodbyes and you don't have to pretend you're going to call him because by the time he wakes up to find you've taken off, he'll be in little doubt as to the message you were trying to get across.

But its downfalls are massive. For a start, as anyone who's ever been on the receiving end of a MF will tell you, it's incredibly hurtful to think that someone who has seen you naked and shared a night of passion with you has concluded that you're such a repulsive and gruesome specimen she can't even bear to be around you when she's unconscious. And on a more practical note, there are many ways in which an MF can go wrong. You can find yourself standing on the street in a crappy part of town where there are no cabs and the local drug dealer approaches you and asks if you're looking for a pimp. This is bad enough when you know where you are, but if you're in a strange area (see "I Don't Know Where I Am," above), it's terrifying. But the most alarming cautionary tale I've ever heard comes from my friend Donna (remember her? The one with the organic boyfriend), who was so desperate to escape the scuzzy studio apartment she'd found herself in that she dashed down the stairs and out of the door as soon as her date had passed out. She slammed the front door behind her, and tried the handle of the porch door—only to find that the porch door was locked, and the front door behind her wasn't budging either. The poor dear spent a cold, miserable eight hours there, during which time she got so desperate for the bathroom she had to pee in a planter. Her conquest eventually found her at ten the next morning. She didn't know what was worse: the shame and guilt at the way she'd treated him, or the fact that after all that shivering on the porch, she still had to face him in the morning.

and beyond...

First off, we want to deal with the immediate aftermath of your date. And that calls for a postmortem—a meeting with three or four of your closest friends, which may or may not involve more food and booze, during which you deconstruct the pros and cons of the date.

My post-date postmortems have included those that were incredibly formal, when three of my friends who had by some amazing coincidence (er, we'd all been in heat at the same party exactly one week before) had also been on first dates the previous night; in anticipation of stories to be shared and love bites to be compared, we booked a table for champagne brunch in a ridiculously expensive London hotel. Then there are the slightly less formal post-date postmortems, like chatting to a trusted colleague by the water cooler. Then there are the downright dishevelled post-date postmortems, like crawling into your roommate's bedroom at 11 on a Sunday morning to muse on life, love and everything while eating last night's delivered pizza in front of the TV.

Whatever form your PD PM takes, it's vital to remember that this isn't only an excuse for you to ramble on about your new guy until your friends' eyes glaze over (although this is, of course, an important part of the process), but also to listen to and inwardly digest what they have got to say. Feedback is essential when it comes to a new man. A postmortem offers a few practical merits—you do, after all, need an objective view from your friends about what kind of guy he is and where the relationship could go from here. Because when you're drunk on lust, you can't always see the situation clearly and rationally. But more than anything else, it's a reminder that while men come and go, girly bonding sessions are for life.

how to get a second date

A follow-up call a couple of days after your date is just good manners and gives you a chance to state where you stand with each other.

Again, unless he was a hideous human being, don't cut off all contact. Even if you agreed to part as friends, it's nice to call him and clear the air and let him know you'd like to stay in touch.

If you've changed your mind about him since your date, a well-timed phone call is the best way to reject him. A good escape clause I've used in the past is "I really enjoyed your company, but an old flame of mine has just come back from Tokyo after a couple of years and we're going to give it another try." It doesn't matter that most of my ex-boyfriends have never left Europe—for some reason, it's less of a blow to be rejected for an ex than it is to be rejected because you're a lame person.

To get a second date, just say what a great time you had and ask him to name an evening in the next week or so when he's free. Use the same tactics you used to pin him down for the first date, but be a little more forceful this time. Take it as a given that you're going to get together again, but it's just a question of when you can fit it in. If he suggests the next evening, hold your horses, bite your tongue and say you can't. You still don't want to be too available because a girl who has to make an effort to fit him in will ALWAYS be more attractive than a girl who abandons all her friends the minute a new man enters the scene. Not only will that scare the bejesus out of him, it's no good for you, either. Funnily enough, friends don't take kindly to being dropped like a hot potato when you get laid.

Sometimes he won't call, or won't return your call, after a date. This is shitty behavior in the extreme. I consider it the height of rudeness to have sex with someone and then just dump her without a word of explanation. But annoyingly, men do this from time to time.

I asked a lot of men why they do this and while a couple of them, predictably and sadly, said that they lost interest in a girl once the thrill of the chase was over, most of them said that more often than not, the man is tying himself up in knots over the follow-up phone call. Apparently, they don't want to call right away in case they seem too eager (you see? You see? They're playing games just as much as we are!), but by the time they think a reasonable amount of time has lapsed, it then occurs to them that perhaps they let it go a little too long and they're embarrassed to make the call after that. This is especially true if the night you spent together was mindblowingly awesome, and the whole experience was so intense they had to take a step back to get their head together. "So in a way," said one male friend, "if you don't call her it's 'cause you really like her and she's had a special effect on you." And they say that men are the ones whose brains work on logic and reason? Hmm.

This came as a bit of a surprise to me, but I was actually quite heartened because even though it shows that men can be quite hopeless, it also gives rise to the hope that they're not all callous bastards and that there are in fact some sensitive souls out there. Working on this premise, now is NOT the time to call him and berate him about his lack of communication. Rather, give him a call and don't mention a follow-up date or hassle him about where he thinks this (still-fledgling) relationship is going. This way, you'll let him off the hook he's been dangling on, let him know it's OK for him to call you whenever he wants, but you're not making life too easy for him. He still needs to suggest the follow-up date, and you couldn't have paved a smoother way for him to do so.

(Needless to say, if he doesn't go on to suggest a second date and isn't receptive to your charming follow-up phone call, he's an idiot and an asshole who doesn't know a good thing when he sees it. You have my express permission to spread the rumor that he has a small penis.)

happily ever after?

After a month or so of dating, you'll be able to work out exactly where you stand with your new guy. If he doesn't turn out to be The One, then chalk him up to experience, part on good terms and start checking out his guy friends. Hopefully you've realized that while it has its ups and downs, the dating game can be fun when you've got the right attitude, the right advice and, perhaps most importantly of all, the right shoes. And if he *does* turn out to your soul mate, then go forth, and good luck—you're on your own from now on. Or rather, you're not….

And by the way, I am able to provide my own transportation to and accommodation at your wedding.

other books by ulysses press

The Little Bit Naughty Book of Sex
Dr. Jean Rogiere, $9.95

A handy pocket hardcover that is a fun, full-on guide to enjoying great sex.

Sexy Bitch's Book of Doing It, Getting It and Giving It
Flic Everett, $9.95

Dishes the dirty truth on everything from foreplay and oral sex to sex toys and fantasy games.

Make Love All Night and Talk to Him in the Morning: Bite-size Tips for Sex and Relationships
Dr. Pam Spurr, $9.95

Explains how to develop sexual techniques, practice safer sex and be a more creative lover; the book also offers suggestions on meeting men, enjoying dates and strengthening a committed relationship.

The Wild Guide to Sex and Loving
Siobhan Kelly, $16.95

Packed with practical, frank and sometimes downright dirty tips on how to hone your bedroom skills, this handbook tells you everything you need to know to unlock the secrets of truly tantalizing sensual play.

To order these books call 800-377-2542 or 510-601-8301, fax 510-601-8307, e-mail ulysses@ulyssespress.com, or write to Ulysses Press, P.O. Box 3440, Berkeley, CA 94703. All retail orders are shipped free of charge. California residents must include sales tax. Allow two to three weeks for delivery.

about the author

SIOBHAN KELLY is the author of *The Wild Guide to Sex and Loving* and a contributing editor for *Cosmopolitan*. She writes extensively on sex and relationships and has contributed to *Company*, *More!*, *Cosmo Girl* and *Sky* magazines.